Walking Out of War

The Eastern Front, Book 3

Scott Bury

Independent Authors International

Walking Out of War
Copyright 2017 by Scott Bury

Createspace edition
ISBN 978-1-987846-05-8

Published by The Written Word Communications Co.,

Ottawa, Ontario, 2017.
An Independent Authors International title.

Cover design by David C. Cassidy
Edited by Gary Henry
Proofread by Joy A. Lorton, Typo-Detective.
Quality control by Independent Authors International

Contents

AS ALWAYS, DEDICATED TO THE
MEMORY OF MAURICE BURY

Written for Roxanne

Prologue:

The Red Army returns

Nastasiv, Ukraine, August 1944

Maurice stepped outside onto his mother's front doorstep. He lit a cigarette, drew a lungful and turned his face upward. He closed his eyes to exhale and savoured the feeling of the sun on his face. It felt like the first day of peace after his nightmarish journey from Kalush.

We have to find somewhere else for Maria to stay. People will notice two extra residents in this house, and we don't want anyone to ask questions.

The air smelled sweet with hay and growing sugar beets. He looked out at his mother's fields. *They're doing well,* he thought. *We'll have a good crop this year.* He crouched, digging his fingers into the rich black soil. He pulled a few weeds out from between the beets.

He stood again, leaned against the fence and closed his eyes. *How much longer will this war last? Germany lost the war in 1941, when they stopped outside Moscow and Leningrad. Now they're gone. And now, Ukraine has to fight Stalin's USSR to be free.*

The Soviets had pushed the Germans out of almost all Ukraine by the end of spring. In June 1944, they had launched Operation Bagration, which had swept the Germans out of Belarus and pushed them away from Leningrad. By August, the Red Army was on the Vistula River in Poland, and the Polish Home Army was fighting the Germans to control Warsaw. Meanwhile, the Americans, British, Free French and Canadians were penetrating deep into German-occupied France. *Germany won't just surrender, though. Hitler is too stubborn.*

Maurice wondered about Ukraine's chances of independence from the USSR. It would be a political question, he knew, dependent on the will of the countries of the West.

And Poland. A free Poland will claim western Ukraine, Russia the east.

Maybe I should go back to Canada when this is over.

Something clamped his left arm, and then something else grabbed his right. He looked up and felt cold terror when he saw the red stripes on the uniforms on the men holding him by the arms: NKVD, Stalin's political police.

"Come with us, comrade," said one as they pulled him toward a covered truck. They threw him in the back, where a handful of other fearful-looking young men sat on the floor under the watch of another soldier with a machine gun ready. The engine roared and the truck lurched. One of the young men fell face down as the truck jolted along.

Maurice knew what this was about. The Red Army needed more men to make up some of the incredible losses of men its victories brought.

At the Nastasiv town hall, the soldiers pushed the young captives into a hall where NKVD soldiers lined all the walls. Slawka, the mayor's daughter whom he had tutored before the war, sat at the reception desk. She watched them come in with wide eyes and open mouth.

Behind a long table, under a huge portrait of Stalin, sat a commissar. Soldiers brought their captives up to him one by one. He took their names and nodded, and soldiers led each one out to another truck to take them to a training camp.

It was Maurice's turn. The commissar looked at him carefully. "How old are you?"

There was no point in lying. "Twenty-five."

"Why aren't you in the army, then, comrade?"

Maurice could not tell them that he already had been in the army, had been captured and then escaped. Explaining that would lead to summary execution for desertion. "I am a teacher in a rural school, exempt from compulsory service."

"Not during wartime," said the commissar.

"I am also working on my mother's farm. I'm the only man in the family."

"I think you're a deserter."

Behind him, Maurice heard Slawka gasp. "Maurice!" she whispered, and he heard her running away.

"No, comrade commissar!" Maurice protested. "No, I was never called up before the Germans invaded, and after that it was too late——"

"You're lying," said the commissar. He only had to look at the NKVD soldiers, and they took Maurice's arms again.

He heard a clatter and then Slawka ran back into the hall with a short, bald man dressed in a rumpled grey suit and tie: her father, Stepan Husar, the mayor. "Please, help him!" said Slawka.

"What's wrong, comrade commissar?" asked the mayor, a little out of breath.

"Nothing you need concern yourself with, comrade," the commissar sneered. "This is an Army matter."

"But why have you arrested this man?" Husar's hair was messed and his tie was crooked. He tried to straighten it, embarrassed under the commissar's glare.

"Do you know him?"

"Maurice? Of course I know him. He's Tekla Kuritsa's son, he teaches in the ridna shkola, and tutors children—for free."

"Goddammit, you liar! This man told me himself he was in UPA. Guards, take him out and shoot him."

Maurice felt cold. His leg began to ache where he had been wounded at Kiev, and he irrationally feared that the pain would give him away—that the commissar would be able to take it as proof that he had served in the army.

"I don't know anything about that," the mayor said, speaking quickly. "I know he's a good man, an intelligent man, loyal. He's never been a nationalist."

"There is no record of him as a teacher before the war," said the commissar.

"We destroyed the records three years ago to keep them out of the Germans' hands," the mayor said.

"What about you?" asked the commissar? "Are you a Party member?"

"Yes."

"Show me your membership card."

"I destroyed it when the Germans came. They would have shot me. I have daughters, comrade commissar."

The commissar drummed his fingers on the table.

"Listen, please, commissar," the mayor continued. "This man is not a nationalist. He's not in UPA, not a spy. I personally vouch for him." Maurice wondered how much of his history Husar actually knew.

"Very well. Put him on the train for Donbass."

This time, there was no time to go home and collect any belongings. Maurice and the other captives were loaded onto a battered, creaking train and were soon on their way east, to another training camp.

This time, Maurice was not an officer, but a private soldier. The Red Army would again send him to fight—and probably die—against Nazi Germany.

Back to training camp

Donbass, summer 1944

"How did you learn to break down a rifle so quickly?" the drill sergeant asked.

"I grew up on a farm," Maurice answered. "You have to have a gun on a farm."

"A shotgun, yes. Not an automatic rifle. I come from a farm, too," said the drill sergeant. He was a small man with a round face and earnest brown eyes.

Maurice shrugged, hoping the sergeant would not hear his hammering heart. "I guess I'm just a fast learner."

The sergeant's eyes narrowed, but he moved on to the boy beside Maurice, who was fumbling with his weapon. "Get that magazine back together in the next sixty seconds or you're on double guard duty tonight!"

I have to be more clumsy. And more careful, at the same time, Maurice thought.

Compared to his experience as an officer three years earlier, this training camp for soldiers was brutal. In August 1944, the Red Army had reached the outskirts of Warsaw and was within sight of the Gulf of Riga. They had pushed the Germans out of Russia, Ukraine and Belorussia and were throwing every man they could find into the drive to destroy Hitler's Germany.

In June, the Red Army had launched Operation Bagration. Two million men, thousands of tanks, heavy assault guns and airplanes, attacked in a coordinated series of attacks along a front that stretched from Estonia to Romania, accompanied by 220,000 trucks from the U.S., with tanks and guns from Britain, tonnes and tonnes of food and ammunition from the West. In two months, they pushed the Germans out of Belorussia.

The Soviets annihilated the German Army Group Center. Hundreds of thousands of German soldiers were killed, wounded and captured, including thirty-one generals—a quarter of the German strength on the Eastern Front gone in two months.

The Red Army's losses, while not as severe, were still huge: 800,000 casualties, including over 180,000 killed and missing.

In August, the communists put Maurice and other men they had rounded up on a train. Two days later, he found himself in a training camp in the Donbas region, the basin of the river Don, famous for coal production and hot summers.

Three years earlier, Maurice had thought that the drill sergeants in the officers' camp were tough. In the camp for enlisted soldiers, the trainers drove the recruits like demons, trying to make them combat-ready in four weeks.

They went on marches for half a day, running much of the time, or dug holes in the ground for no reason.

Maurice was a little better off than the raw recruits. With his previous officer experience, he knew what the drill sergeants wanted. Sometimes too well.

Most of the new recruits were very young, the last remaining boys from the farms and villages across Ukraine, those unlucky enough to reach their seventeenth birthdays before the war ended.

Not all were young, though. Old Stepan was in his forties, and Maurice wondered sometimes if Stepan's story wasn't similar to his own. But Stepan obviously had no experience with weapons or army life, and could not keep up with boys half his age.

One very hot day, the sergeant assigned Maurice, Stepan and eight young boys to pull an obsolete heavy cannon up a hill. They knew better by this time than to grumble. Four boys put leather straps over their shoulders and pulled; Maurice and another got behind to push, leaving Stepan and the remaining boys to pull a wagon of ammunition. With the sun beating down on them and the humidity making every breath a chore, they hauled the massive gun across a muddy field to the bottom of the hill. The wheels squeaked and stuck, then sank into the mud.

"Get moving, you lazy buggers!" the sergeant yelled. "You think Fritz is going to wait for you to get your lazy asses moving? You'd all be dead a hundred times over by now on the battlefield!"

Maurice wondered if the sergeant had ever been to the battlefield, and decided that, in all likelihood, he had. There was almost no one left in Ukraine or Russia now who hadn't been scarred in some way.

So they pushed and pulled the gun across the mud, trying as much as possible to stay on grass so the wheels wouldn't sink so much into the ground. The sergeant had chosen their route to be as difficult as possible.

Halfway up the hill, the wheels stopped turning. The boys paused barely long enough to determine that the cause was too much mud caked around the axles before the sergeant was screaming at them again to keep moving. "The fucking Germans aren't so polite they'll let you clean up! Your comrades are dying on top of that hill unless you get that gun up there! Get moving, you fucking little girls!" Pushing the cannon became dragging the cannon.

It was nearly noon by the time they got the gun to the top of the low hill. Their uniforms were soaked and caked with dust. All the boys fell onto the ground, exhausted.

"Get up!" said the sergeant. The heat was getting to him, too: his shirt was wet with sweat and he wasn't raising his voice anymore. "The Germans have retreated. Take this gun back to the base."

The boys couldn't help groaning, but the sergeant let that pass. They all stood up wearily and picked up the straps. Only Stepan stayed on the ground.

"Won't you join us, comrade?" the sergeant sneered.

"I can't," Stepan puffed. "I'm worn out."

The sergeant pulled his pistol from its holster. "Get up, you lazy son of a bitch, or I'll shoot you right now!"

Eyes wide, Stepan got up, picked up a box of ammunition and led the troop down the hill.

Liberating Estonia

On the train to Finland

September 1944

Three years to the day after the launch of Operation Barbarossa, the USSR launched its largest offensive of the war: Operation Bagration. Despite pleas from the western Allies to time the attack to coincide with D-Day on June 6, the Stavka, the supreme command in Moscow, had stuck to their symbolic date of June 22.

A month later, Ivan Konev's First Ukrainian Front began the Lvov-Sandomierz Offensive to drive the Germans out of the last bit of Ukraine and eastern Poland.

The operation began with the Soviet military strategy called *maskirovka*, or deception. While the German high command made four contingency plans for likely Soviet offensives, the Stavka moved forces and leaked information to trick the Germans into diverting their already depleted forces from Poland and Romania into Belorussia.

Bagration launched simultaneously along a front that stretched thousands of miles from the Baltic to Belorussia. By the end of July, the Red Army had reached the Gulf of Riga, splitting the German Army Group North and Army Group Centre. The Germans counterattacked and managed to create a short-lived corridor between the two groups, but ultimately the forces in Estonia and Latvia were cut off.

Meanwhile, Stalin renewed attacks on Finland in June, hoping to knock it out of the war so the Red Army could concentrate on the drive to Berlin. The Stavka sent fresh resources to the newly liberated Leningrad, and from there to the Karelian Isthmus. The Finns fought the Soviets to a virtual standstill through the summer and into September, 1944.

Maurice looked out the window at a scene that brought his mind back three years. He remembered peering out a narrow opening in a freight car hurriedly converted to carrying troops, seeing row after row of train tracks, wagons filled with soldiers and weapons, the city of Kyiv burning behind all that.

That time, he had been an officer, fresh out of the academy in Akhtyrka in eastern Ukraine. He remembered how the train carrying the disorganized, demoralized Red Army had pulled into Kyiv that was already under attack. Operation Barbarossa was the greatest land invasion in history, and the Red Army reeled back from it, suffering hundreds of thousands of casualties. The Germans took millions of prisoners, whole armies.

Maurice unconsciously rubbed his knee where shrapnel had torn into it that summer day in 1941. He thought, though, of those 11 men he had commanded in 1941. They had been an anti-tank squad, but their weapons had been no match for the Panzer. They had retreated before the onslaught almost all the way across Ukraine, until they were captured along with millions of other men near Kharkiv. Then the greatest stroke of luck in his life. One of the officers in charge of the prison camp was a man he knew. A Ukrainian who had joined the Germans, believing the false promise of "freedom for all nations" from communist oppression. His name was Bohdan, but when he joined the German Army, he changed his name to Daniel. And he took an immense chance in freeing his old friend, along with the 11 men in his command.

Where is Daniel now? Is he alive or dead? Will I ever learn?

Now, in 1944, he peered out the window of a car that was actually fitted for transporting troops, with seats and real windows. For a moment, he looked at his pale reflection in the glass. He had always been slim as a youth, but now he was thin, hardened by nearly four years of war and espionage. There were the beginnings of little lines around his expressive brown eyes. The wave in the front of his hair, of which he had once been proud, somehow persisted, but now he thought it a futile display, like a peacock's feathers when facing a man with a shotgun.

His attention went back outside as the train rolled into the rail yard, a broad expanse of sidings and switches. Behind them, the ruins of Leningrad, a city that was once the envy of Europe. Smoke rose above the city, and Maurice wondered whether it was a factory or a fire.

"This is it. The last stop before Finland," said Mykhailo Boyko, another Ukrainian conscript in Maurice's *odalenye,* or company. He was a short, chubby, soft young man, 21 years old, with fair hair that always looked greasy. "Those damn Finns are tough. Do you know that they killed five Russians for every one of theirs they lost?"

"Shut up," said Taras Kuchnir, a slender eighteen-year-old from Kalush. "I don't need to hear you tell us how unbeatable the Finns are."

"It's just that—" Mykhailo began.

"I know. Now shut the fuck up," Taras said.

Maurice leaned toward the others, and they leaned closer to hear him. "Keep your heads down, boys. Don't be heroes. Shoot when it makes a difference. We can all survive this."

The train slowed. The boys looked at each other and straightened, checking over their shoulders for commissars. Instead, a senior sergeant entered from the next car and blew a whistle. "Ready to disembark. Get your weapons and gear ready." He reached the end of the car and went through the little door to the next one.

The train stopped at the platform and the men picked up their packs, rifles and company gear, then climbed down to a sea of men, horses, wagons hauling field guns and tanks, trucks honking, non-commissioned officers shouting and NKVD military police blowing whistles.

"This way, men," called Maurice's sergeant, a tough, dedicated Communist Russian named Nikolai Nikolaev. Close to six feet, he was taller than Maurice, and fit. When he rolled up his sleeves, his long arms reminded Maurice of heavy rope. "We get a meal and a rest and then we get on another train for the Finnish front."

They climbed down to the platform and joined the rest of their company, commanded by Captain Ilya Baranov and Commissar Alex Sorkin. Baranov was a barrel-chested young man, no more than 25 years old, with dark brown hair and eyes, and white scars across his cheeks and on the backs of his hands. Sorkin was thin, compact, his uniform with its red patches perfectly clean and pressed. Like every officer, he carried a sidearm in a leather holster on his hip, and Maurice suspected a copy of the Communist Manifesto in his pocket.

Try as they might, Baranov and Sorkin could not move the company through the press of the Red Army. From one side, another regiment moved across their path. On the other side, porters loaded guns and equipment onto horse-drawn wagons. Men pressed shoulders, squeezing past Maurice and Mykhailo.

Maurice looked around the train station. The main station building had been nearly wiped out by German bombs. There was no glass in the tall, proud windows, no roof except for planks put up temporarily. Exposed beams made the roundhouse and outbuildings look like skeletons of ancient monsters. Beyond the press of men and vehicles, Maurice could see piles of rubble pushed to the sides of the streets. At one corner, old men and women held ragged coats closed at their throats and watched the army disembarking.

After standing in place for a half-hour, the company was finally able to move with the rest of the regiment. They shuffled down the platform, squeezing between another regiment on one side and a burned-out building on the other to emerge into a square. *The whole city looks grey, like ash,* Maurice thought. The bright sunlight only accentuated the burn marks and the craters in the streets.

The regiment trooped into a huge, open building that looked like a massive barn. Long tables ran the length of it, and men went to the far end to line up for a meal.

Maurice sat down across from Mykhailo. Taras was beside him, and Young Olesh—not the youngest man in the company, but with a remarkable baby face with full cheeks and not a trace of facial hair—on the other side. Borys Kozak sat across the table from him. He was a thin man in his mid-twenties, like Maurice, but from a village far from the front lines, hundreds of kilometres east of Kyiv.

"I love this American ham," Maurice said. Beside a slice of ham taken from a can was a scoop of buckwheat porridge, called kasha, and a spoonful of canned peas. *All supplied by the British and Americans. What a difference from the beginning of the war.*

Mykhailo could not stop talking about the Finns. "Do you know we lost five times as many men in 1939 as the Finns did?" he said again. "The USSR sent everything they had into Karelia: tanks, men, planes, ships, everything. The Finns gave up a few kilometres of territory. And now, they're supplied by the Germans. German guns, tanks, planes, everything." His voice dropped and he leaned closer to the others. "I heard they have ghost soldiers that can go through snow and ice to kill Russians."

"Those were just men in white uniforms and skis," Maurice scoffed. "Don't believe every old wives' tale you hear."

"They're still very tough fighters. And the snow is going to be very deep. That's going to be a killer for us just as it was for the Germans in 1942," said Young Olesh.

"It's September," said Serhiy Koval, who had come with Olesh from western Ukraine. The two had been inseparable in training camp and ever since. "Maybe there won't be snow in Finland yet."

"There won't be any more snow in southern Finland than there is here in Leningrad," Maurice said. He took a big bite of his ham and let the others argue about how tough and unbeatable the Finns were. When he swallowed, he looked at the others around him, then down the table to Sergeant Nikolaev. He was talking with the lieutenant, an earnest, blond Russian named Vasilyev. *Good. He won't hear me.*

"The Red Army today isn't the same as the Red Army in 1941," he said. He knew he had to be careful not to give the men any idea that he had been in the Red Army in 1941. "Now, we have American food, British guns and cannons, American and British made tanks, American trucks, American cigarettes." He took out a cigarette and lit it. "In 1941, the USSR had next to nothing—no food, bad uniforms. Boots wore off the soldiers' feet as they were retreating." He lifted his foot onto the bench to show off his new, American-made boot with leather foot and canvas upper. "Look at that. Not as good as what the officers have, but much better than they used to be."

"How do you know all this?" Young Olesh asked.

Maurice hid the alarm the question made him feel. "The thing is, when you're fighting, fear is your worst enemy. Panic makes you forget your training, it makes you make mistakes. And that is what gets you killed."

"Have you ever been in a war before, Maurice?" Young Olesh asked, and Maurice felt like hitting him.

"No, of course not. I'm a new draftee as much as you are."

"Really? You seem to know a lot about fighting. And you're the fastest in the odalenye at breaking down your rifle."

Maurice forced a smile he hoped looked real. "I just pay attention to the training."

Young Olesh did not look convinced. Worse, neither did Mykhailo. *If I can't convince a dummy like Myko, I'm in trouble.*

An hour later, they marched back to the train station. It was a different platform than the one where they had arrived, but it was still just as crowded and chaotic. A major and a staff sergeant stood on a wagon, shouting orders and pointing regiments one way and another.

A train waited on the track, doors open. Men unloaded heavy crates while two generals argued, yelling at each other on the platform in front of it. Maurice could not hear what they were saying above the din of the platform.

Sergeant Nikolaev ordered a halt. "What's going on?" Mykhailo asked.

"Something about new orders," said Corporal Shewchuk, Nikolaev's second-in-command, a tall and serious-faced man from Vinnytsia, Ukraine. He squinted at the arguing generals in front of the train. "It seems we're not going to Finland anymore."

"We're not?" It was hard to tell whether Mykhailo felt relieved or more frightened. "Why? What happened?"

"Cease-fire," said a corporal in another regiment on the platform. "Finland and the USSR are going to sign an armistice."

"We beat the Finns?" Mykhailo asked.

The corporal shrugged. "Guess so. Now we can concentrate on Germany."

Two days later, the regiment rode another train southwest. Through the window, Maurice watched the farmland and shattered towns of the Leningrad Oblast. It seemed not a building remained intact. The railroad went through towns that had been entirely leveled.

When the train passed a station with a sign that read Narva, Maurice realized they had reached Estonia, which the Germans called Ostland. Its history was complex. Home to a sizable German elite minority for centuries, Estonia had been independent after the fall of the Russian Empire during the Great War. In 1939, the Molotov-von Ribbentrop Pact ceded the Baltic states to the Soviet "sphere of influence," and Germany evacuated tens of thousands of ethnic Germans from Estonia and Latvia before the Soviets took over. The Soviets deported thousands of Estonians to Siberia and killed thousands more.

When Germany invaded in 1941, many Estonians saw it as a liberator from Stalin, as many had in Ukraine. And as in Ukraine, the hopes for independence were soon proven to be lies. Germany set up Reichskommissariat Ostland, a huge buffer zone between "greater Germany" and the occupied areas of the USSR. Nazi Germany confiscated all the state property that the Soviets had confiscated a year earlier and imprisoned or killed the Estonian political, intellectual and commercial leaders that had not escaped. The German Reich minister for the occupied eastern territories began "germanizing" Estonia, Latvia and Lithuania. The Nazis set up concentration camps and murdered tens of thousands of Estonians, including over 4,000 Jews. By the end of 1944, the Reichskommissar could declare Ostland "Jew-free." The Nazis exploited Estonia's resources for their war effort and used Estonians as slave labour.

Which means the country is filled with partisans fighting both the USSR and Germany. Just like Ukraine.

As evening fell, the train stopped at an improvised army base, a muddy field in the midst of forests. The crops that had once grown there had been burned by war and churned by vehicles and marching feet. A few trees still held leaves, colourful in the fall, but most had been blackened and broken. Skeletal ruins of a town and farm buildings were grey against the red sunset.

"The Estonian-Latvian border is ten kilometres west of here," said the earnest Lieutenant Vasilyev. "The Germans hold the border town of Valga. We're going to take it in the morning."

Maurice looked at Mykhailo. He was shaking. Old Stepan looked glum, as usual, and Young Olesh was pale even in the red sunset.

Maurice took a deep breath and let it out slowly. *I've been in action. I've been in far worse situations, when we were running from the Germans. I survived. I will survive tomorrow, too.*

They camped, groups of three making little tents of their *chenilles*, or greatcoats: one on the ground, two draped over their rifles, propped up as poles. They would sleep alongside one another in shifts: every few hours, they would change around, so each of the three had a few hours in between the other two, and thus the warmest place in the tent.

The sergeants woke them quietly before dawn. They packed their gear, pulling on their greatcoats against the chill. Maurice tightened his helmet strap and checked his rifle magazine was full. The sergeant led them to their starting position. Groups of two *odalenye*, or twenty-four in total, would accompany a tank. "Let the tank do the hard work," said Nikolaev. "Your job is to protect it from enemy infantry. The tank will be your protection, but remember that it's also the target for Fritz's artillery. In the town, watch the windows and don't trust the civilians. A lot of partisans favour the Nazis and will kill any socialist comrade they can."

Or maybe they just want to be free from both Germany and Russia, Maurice thought. "Keep low, boys, and keep your eyes focused ahead for Fritz in hiding places," he told his comrades.

The Lieutenant stepped in front of them. "This is our first experience in carrying out deep operations. The shock army will hit as soon as there's light. Keep your head down as the planes strike. The tanks will move fast, striking deep. We're the second echelon," he said, and Maurice thought he sounded disappointed. "When they've broken through, we follow into the breach and occupy the town, destroy any remaining resistance and take over their bases, ammunition, vehicles. Our regiment's specific objective is the railroad station. When we get there, we'll set up the Maxim as a defensive weapon. If the enemy counterattacks, follow your training. Fire in short bursts. Don't waste ammunition."

A colonel stepped up behind Lieutenant Vasileyev, his battle uniform perfect. "We're going to liberate Valga today," he said, catching each man's eye in turn. "That means we are freeing Latvia from the Nazi tyrant, restoring the rule of the people of the Soviet Socialist Republic of Latvia, and tomorrow, Lithuania as well. Other than partisans, this town is part of the Soviet Union. Stavka will not tolerate looting or abuse of the civilian population. Is that understood?" He did not wait for a reply, but walked away to repeat his message to the next group.

Sergeant Nikolaev summed it up. "Hands off the women and especially the girls."

The sky lightened behind them, and then a line of planes buzzed past overhead. Maurice had faced the blitzkrieg in 1941. He knew what it was to be overwhelmed by a fast, unstoppable foe.

But nothing could have prepared him for the Red Army's assault on the German invaders in 1944. The line of planes hitting the enemy stretched in both directions as far as he could see, and explosions lit up the western horizon with a hellish light. They felt the earth vibrating, felt the heat on their faces.

As the sun's first rays lit up the field, Maurice saw the artillery raise their barrels and begin firing: mortars and cannons, long-range artillery pieces and something new: the Guards Mortars, the innovative rocket launchers that became known as the Katyusha. They looked like the pipes of a church organ mounted on cantilevered assembly on the back of one of the now-ubiquitous Studebaker trucks. Maurice watched a crew load fourteen metre-long rockets onto the rails. The rails rose, pointing at an upward angle toward the enemy. Then with an unbearably loud but almost musical sound, they fired. Rows of multiple rocket launchers sent a volley of thousands of shells toward the Germans. *Nothing could survive that,* Maurice thought.

Then the shock armies raced westward. First came tanks and armoured cars, all carrying men with a grim but confident air. Looking at them, Maurice knew they had no illusions that some of them were going to die, but they were going to destroy the enemy.

Hundreds of vehicles poured past Maurice's position. The Germans returned fire, but that did not slow the shock troops. As the day brightened, the men could see the German positions in the town of Valga, about two kilometres to the west. Smoke billowed up from dozens of spots. Buildings crumbled as shells from Soviet tanks and cannon struck.

Successive lines of Soviet tanks, trucks, guns and men moved across the fields toward the first buildings of the town. Men fell, trucks burst into smoke and fire but the shock troops kept moving forward.

And then, the returning fire stopped. Maurice could see the Red Army moving fast down a road away from him, like a sink draining. Another wave of planes screeched past overhead, flying past the town and bombing the distance.

"Ahead, boys!" Sergeant Nikolaev called. Maurice and the men picked up their automatic rifles. Four pulled the Pulemyot Maxima machine gun. Although the lieutenant and the men called it the "Maxim," it was actually a Russian-made variant of the original Maxim heavy machine gun. Mounted on a two-wheeled carriage, it had a high shield and a special cap for water to cool it. It required at least two to operate it: one to load the belts of ammunition, and one to aim and fire. It was mostly used for defending against counterattacks.

Ahead, Maurice saw Red Army men jump up and climb on the decks of the T-34s, squat behind the turret and aim their rifles, but he stayed on the ground, thinking of the lieutenant's warning that the tanks would be the Germans' main targets.

When they reached the burned forest, they had to follow the road. A single tank led three odalenyes. Taking his turn to help pull the Maxim, Maurice felt vulnerable, squeezed among so many men concentrated onto the road. One shell would kill this whole unit. But no shells fell. They could hear explosions and fighting ahead of them. They passed a metal sign, bent and punctured by bullets, reading *Valga*. Other than the grinding and clanking of the tanks and the sound of marching feet, the morning was now quiet.

They had to get off the road where a crater made it impassable, exactly where it crossed a railway. "Fritz blew that as they were retreating," said Corporal Shewchuk. Six men struggled to pull the Maxim over the soft ground beside the road.

A burning house on the left side of the road marked the beginning of the town. Smoke poured from a hole in its roof. Fifty metres ahead, at an intersection with a side street, stood what looked like the remains of an inn, its walls blackened and scarred.

The tank moved ahead and the men spread out as much as they could. Maurice heard a crack and the man beside him screamed and fell, clutching his leg. Another crack and a man dropped from the tank deck to the ground and did not move any more.

Maurice dropped to the ground. "Sniper in the inn!" Nikolaev called. A dozen Soviet rifles chattered and Maurice saw chips fly off the wall around a first-storey window. More cracks answered, but without visible effect.

The tank's turret swiveled and the cannon roared. The top of the inn disappeared in a flash and a burst of smoke and splinters. Seconds later, three men in grey uniforms ran out of the ruins of the inn, weaponless, hands high in the air. Soviet guns barked and the three men dropped, dead.

They were surrendering, Maurice thought. *Why did we shoot?* Then he realized that he was squeezing the trigger of his own rifle. *I shot. Did I hit one of them?* He could not know.

The tank moved on. Maurice stood up and followed it, along with the other men in his odalenye. They trotted to keep up and entered the town.

Not a building was left undamaged. Bullets had scarred every wall that was still standing. Houses had collapsed, shops crumbled. The road was choked with rubble and bodies in German uniforms and civilian clothing.

Amid houses and shops, Maurice felt more vulnerable than ever before. He and the boys tried to look in all directions at once. Every window and doorway could conceal a German sniper or a Latvian partisan.

"This way, men," shouted an officer, leading them down a side street. The company picked their way past the rubble of shattered houses and shops. They worked their way carefully past blasted civilian cars and trucks. More civilian bodies lay in the street. Young Olesh cried out a little when he saw a young mother and a small girl sprawled in a doorway. They heard fighting somewhere ahead, chattering rifles and barking cannons. The air was filled with smoke and falling ash, and the smell of burning wood, rubber and flesh.

Maurice saw a flicker of movement in the corner of his eye and turned toward a dark alley between two houses. Someone else fired, hitting a wall. A small black dog yelped and ran out of the alley and down the street where the Soviets had come from.

The street they were on ended a block away, where another intersected from the right. Smoke billowed around the corner and the sound of fighting was louder. They heard submachine guns and rifles crackling, and then a deep boom, followed by a crash. A thick plume of smoke rose over the building in front of them.

At Sergeant Nikolaev's hand signal, the men pressed against the low brick building on their right. Nikolaev peeked around the corner, then waved the men on as he ran around it.

Maurice and his comrades looked down a short street lined with low shops that opened into a square. In the square were the broken stumps of trees. Red Army soldiers lay dead or crouched behind burned vehicles and broken masonry, firing their rifles across the square. At the far end was a mobile field gun. Its barrel, pointed across the square, was still smoking. Behind it lay the carcasses of the horses that had hauled it.

Across the square, the town's train station belched smoke through its main entrance doors. From second-storey windows, Maurice could see rifle barrels and could hear rattling submachine gun fire.

The field gun fired again and two windows on the second storey vanished into smoke and dust. Maurice heard rumbling as the wall below them collapsed and spilled brick, masonry, timber and glass onto the square. When the smoke cleared, he saw two bodies in grey uniforms among the wreckage.

The gunfire from the train station had ceased. The Red soldiers fired another volley as Maurice, Corporal Shewcuk and Mykhailo Boyko aimed the Maxim. Maurice readied the ammunition belt as Shewchuk aimed. For a few seconds, the only sounds he could hear were the rapid breathing of frightened soldiers and the soft sounds of a fire burning somewhere inside the station. Far off, they could hear more gunfire and the occasional explosion of fighting somewhere else in the town.

Something moved at the hole where the train station's main entrance used to be. "White flag," someone called. "Come out, Fritz!" he called, and then repeated it in German: "Raus!"

The improvised flag waved again, and a Soviet officer called "Raus" again. A face appeared at the door of the train station, then a form. A man stepped forward, hands up, waving a white cloth frantically.

"Civilian," said a Soviet soldier. "Come forward, comrade. Men, hold your fire."

The man was small, thin, grey-haired and dressed in civilian clothes. As he stepped into the square, more people staggered out of the smoke: two more men and a barefoot woman with a torn skirt and ragged coat.

A sergeant stepped forward, rifle aimed at the civilians. "Put your hands on your heads," he ordered, then demonstrated when he saw they did not understand Russian. He grabbed the first man by the lapel of his jacket and pulled him to the side of the square. The others followed until more Soviet soldiers took them by the arms and pushed them across the square. They made them stand against the wall of a burned restaurant.

"How many left inside?" the sergeant demanded of the first man out of the station. He repeated it in German.

"I don't know, sir," the old man whined. "There were not many of us left in the town. Maybe three or four inside, still, if they're still alive. Please, let them come out if they are. The building is on fire."

"How many soldiers were in there?" When the old man shrugged, the sergeant leaned into his face and yelled "How many Nazi soldiers?"

"Th-there were ten this morning. I saw two die when you started shooting, another when the doors collapsed. There were some upstairs, too, but I don't know how many are still alive."

The sergeant nodded to a corporal, who gathered a group of men. An odalenye, 11 men, ran across the square and flattened themselves against the wall of the station. The corporal looked in quickly, pulled back, waited a beat. Nothing happened. He nodded at the men with him and then jumped over the wreckage on the ground into the station. Maurice heard a gunshot. The other men followed him in, shouting "Red Army!"

Young Olesh rose from his crouching position beside Maurice and stretched his long legs. "Get down, you idiot,"

Maurice said. "Are you trying to get shot?" Olesh crouched down again, looking afraid, but nothing happened.

They waited. Olesh panted, and Old Stepan lay on his stomach, bent around the corner of a building, watching the train station, a long low building that had once been yellow. After a while, the corporal came out of the station building, pushing a uniformed middle-aged man ahead of him. The man's head was bleeding and he stumbled and limped as the corporal pushed him to the square, where Captain Baranov met him. "This is the station master, comrade captain," the corporal said. "I found him hiding under his desk."

"Name?"

"Kork," the man said. His voice was hoarse and cracked, and his chin trembled.

"A German," the corporal said. He raised his rifle to the station master's head.

"Nein, nein," the station master whined. "I am unarmed. I surrender."

"You are a combatant," Captain Baranov said. "Consider yourself a prisoner of war." He turned to Lieutenant Vasilyev. "Lieutenant, you and your men will be responsible for the prisoners until the NKVD arrive."

"Yes, comrade captain," Vasilyev replied. "Men, come with me."

Maurice stood and aimed his rifle at the prisoners against the wall. Stepan and Olesh copied him. Corporal Shewchuk and Sergeant Nikolaev began to search them, patting them down. Shewchuck was enjoying patting the woman's body. She cried quietly, tears washing streaks in the ash and soot on her cheeks. When Shewchuck squeezed her breasts, she whimpered.

Nikolayev looked up from where he was checking the pants-legs of the station master. "Hands off the women, corporal. Orders."

"Come on, sarge. Just a little fun here."

Nikolaev stood and hit Shewchuk on the back of the head with his rifle. "You heard the orders, corporal. Hands off the women. Do that again and I'll shoot you." He turned to the other men. "Any of you get any ideas about the women in this country and you'll get the same thing. This is war, not fun and games."

The sounds of fighting died away. Another odalenye went into the station and came out. "It's clear. We found six dead Germans, and there's probably more bodies under the rubble," he reported to the captain. "There are several wrecked wagons in the rail yard on the other side, but nothing serviceable."

An hour later, a colonel arrived with a company of NKVD guards. He organized a parade to the town square, and led the company that escorted the German prisoners, followed by the shock army troops that had overrun the Germans, and then the second-echelon troops.

Maurice and his odalenye were assigned to patrolling the parade's path and checking the buildings and the side streets for any stray German soldiers left behind, as well as local partisans who opposed the USSR. "Check every window, especially on the second floor," Sergeant Nikolaev warned.

They did not find any partisans, but rounding a corner into a side street off the main square, Maurice and Mykhailo saw three men running out of the ruins of a shop, arms overflowing with cans of food. "Halt!" they called in Russian, then in German.

The men took off down the street. Mykhailo ran after them, and after a second's hesitation, Maurice followed. Desperate, the looters ran like deer until one tripped over rubble on the street and sprawled. Cans bounced and rolled, some spilling open. The man called after his comrades, but they disappeared into the growing gloom.

Mykhailo reached him first and pointed his rifle at his head. Maurice reached him a second later. "Don't shoot him," he said.

"We're supposed to shoot looters," Mykhailo said, squinting down his rifle barrel at the Estonian man, who had risen to his knees and was shaking.

Maurice pushed Mykhailo's rifle away. "You heard him. Our orders are to shoot anyone we catch looting. Tell everyone you know that the Red Army is here. That means order. And the next time we see anyone taking anything that doesn't belong to them, we will shoot. Understood?"

The man nodded and stood. As he turned to follow his friends, Mykhailo gave him a solid kick to the rear end. "Don't forget it!" The man stumbled and nearly fell again, but then ran as fast as he could around the first corner.

"It's a good thing the sergeant isn't here," said Mykhailo.

"Come on, let's get back to the parade," Maurice answered.

That evening, the Red Army set up a camp in a farmer's field just outside the town, along the banks of a creek. Maurice sat by a small fire to warm his hands. Next to him, Evhen Marchuk, who had been a law student in Kalush before he was drafted, was beginning to shake. "Cold?" Maurice asked.

"N-no," Evhen answered. "It's just... the fighting, you know? So many close calls today. That inn by the road, the soldiers in the train station. We could have been killed so many times." His shoulders convulsed and his whole body shivered before he could control himself.

"Better get used to it," said Taras, sitting across the fire from him. "There's a long war ahead."

Maurice thought of the fighting three years earlier, when he had been an officer in the Red Army's retreat from the blitzkrieg of Operation Barbarossa. He was trying to think of something to say to comfort Evhen a little, when he was startled to see Lieutenant Vasilyev standing by the fire.

The senior officers had taken beds in the few houses that still stood, but Lieutenant Vasilyev had come to his men in the night. "Keep the fires small," he said. "The countryside is full of partisans. They call themselves the Forest Brothers and they're viciously anti-communist." The men did not say anything until the lieutenant pulled a bottle of Russian brandy from inside his coat. "You men did well today. No, you performed perfectly. I have to say I'm very proud. Now, let's all share a little brandy. Don't get drunk, mind you. We're probably going to be fighting again tomorrow."

And they passed the bottle from man to man. With twelve thirsty mouths, the bottle was soon empty.

That was a much better way to calm Evhen than anything I could have said.

Maurice and the truck

Latvia, October 1944

Maurice paused long enough to push mud off his boot with his rifle butt. The felt upper part of the boot was still filthy, but at least with its leather lower part clean, the boot was lighter.

"Keep up, Bury," Sergeant Nikolaev growled, and Maurice moved a little faster to catch up to his place in line. He felt as if the troop had been chasing the Germans across half of Latvia, but the continuous drizzle prevented anyone from seeing more than a hundred metres ahead. The boys had griped about the rain most of the morning, and then settled into a sullen funk that sank steadily through the day. The men only grumbled when it was their turn to pull the Maxim.

The leaves had fallen from the few trees still standing after years of warfare, and looked dead and depressing. As the Soviets had done three years earlier, the retreating Germans had burned everything behind them. *The Germans are so much more thorough than we were*, Maurice thought. They had burned ripe fields to stubble and ash, burned houses too, wrecked trucks and left animal carcasses to rot. When Hitler ordered them to leave nothing behind the Soviets could use, they made certain of it.

By sundown, the troop still had seen no sign of the Germans. Not even a plane had flown by. The Colonel called the troop to a halt. Stepan slumped down on a stump, all that remained of a shelled tree, and wiped rain from his face. "Miserable day."

Young Olesh came up beside them. "I'm soaked through. This uniform is lousy."

Maurice did not dare to say aloud what he was thinking. He felt the cold deep in his arms and legs. His jaw ached from clenching his teeth so they would not chatter.

But this is much better than it was three years ago. Then, our uniforms were rotten, falling off the men. The only replacements were from taking slightly less damaged clothes from your dead comrades. Officers had good leather boots, but the men had just felt boots that wore out until they had to wrap their feet in old newspapers.

We didn't even have enough ammunition—not that any of it was any use against the Panzer.

He remembered the weeks of retreating to trenches dug by local inhabitants; how they would dig in, how the Luftwaffe dropped bombs precisely where they'd kill as many Reds as possible, how the Soviet shells bounced off the Panzers' armour. He thought of the few times a shell found a vulnerable spot and destroyed a German tank.

How many tanks did I destroy? Three?

He thought of all the young Ukrainian and Russian men dead on the fields, how they had to leave those bodies on the ground to retreat again, moving at night, terrified at the sound of an engine because they knew it had to be German.

And then, the capture. Five whole armies encircled and taken prisoner at once. Hundreds of thousands of men crammed into an ancient castle, starved and worked to death.

I got out, and I got my men out, too. All thanks to Bohdan. And where is he now? Wounded, dead? Killed by one of those freed prisoners from Kharkiv?

And he knew he could not speak a word of this to anyone in the Red Army, because that would mean he was a deserter—he had not reported for duty when the Soviets came back to Ukraine.

Three years later, the men had new uniforms. Their boots were still cloth, but at least they could be replaced when they wore out. They all had weapons and ammunition.

And thousands of trucks. All courtesy—literally—of the Americans, who had shipped hundreds of Studebaker trucks for the Red Army. Maurice marveled at the number of American-made implements used by the proletariat's army: rifles, pistols, bullets, clothes, canned food. For their moral inferiority, the capitalists could deliver a lot of goods.

The Red Army now had tanks, too—the vaunted, Russian-made T-34. Lighter and faster than the monstrous Stalin tank of the early war, the tank that towered two stories above the soldiers and dominated the field of battle until it sank into the mud. The T-34 would later be called the best tank of the war, and it outclassed the Germans' Panzers—even the Tigers.

Maurice took out his pack of cigarettes from his inside pocket. They were damp, too, but he managed to light one and held the match for Stepan to light his, too. *Even our cigarettes have to come from America. And they're better than Russian cigarettes, too.*

"Dig in, boys," said a sergeant from another company. "Captain wants you to raise a berm along here," he swept his arm along, indicating a line from a stand of burnt trees to a blasted barn. "Four men stand watch behind it at a time. The rest can sleep in what's left of that barn." He left to order other men to raise temporary, rudimentary defenses on the other side of the little camp.

The men shoveled and made a low dike with a shallow moat in front of it, good enough to hide behind and protect them against bullets. A lieutenant took three other men into the barn's roofless loft as lookouts, even though they would not be able to see anything on this rainy night.

The berm complete, Maurice and a few other men set up the Maxim behind it and then huddled in the slightly dryer lee of a burned shed to eat their mobile rations. "Even our food comes from America," he muttered, and surprised himself when he realized he had spoken aloud.

"Those cowboys know how to cook, too," said another young soldier that Maurice did not know. He opened his tin can of rations. "This ham is very tasty."

"It's better than what we used to get," said Maurice. *Damn. I shouldn't have said that.*

"What did you used to get?" asked Taras around a mouthful of food.

"Just the Russian garbage. Sometimes, it was just stale bread."

"When was that?"

Think fast, Maurice. "During training. The food was crap in the Donbas."

The others nodded as if that made sense, and Maurice stifled a relieved sigh.

"Think the war will be over soon? Fritz is on the run," said the man who liked the ham.

"It's still a long way to Germany, and Hitler doesn't want to give up any land," Serhiy Koval said.

"France has been liberated, Belgium and Luxembourg too, and I heard that the Canadians have entered Holland," said the ham lover. "Bulgaria and Hungary have turned against Germany, too. Germany can't last."

Maurice laughed bitterly. France had been liberated, or most of it, anyway. Italy soon would be completely free of Hitler. But what about Latvia? Estonia had declared itself a free country when the Red Army drove the Germans out, but its government had to flee the Soviets, too. Latvia would soon be firmly in Stalin's grip.

And Ukraine? The Red Army had rolled across its flat fields in a matter of months, rolling up the Germans almost as quickly as the Germans had taken the country in 1941. Ternopyl had been destroyed in the fighting. The fall of Hitler's empire would be the rise of Stalin's.

A truck groaned up to the barn and parked for the night. The driver got out and three other men jumped out of the back and started unloading. Maurice shivered and felt water seeping through the canvas uppers of his boots. He looked longingly at the truck's cabin. He thought fleetingly of climbing in the back once it was unloaded, but did not want to risk an officer's ire. Instead, he walked up to the front of the truck and leaned against the grill. The engine's damp heat suffused him, strengthened him. He closed his eyes and tilted his head back, thinking deliberately of his mother's kitchen, of Katerina's bed, of warm sunshine on the hills. For a delicious minute, he was no longer at war, but studying again beside his sister Hanya, sitting by the pietsch, his huge cat on his lap, a heavy book balanced on the table.

It couldn't last. The sergeant walked into the barn, turning slightly as he passed Maurice. "Bury, you're on first watch. Get up to the line." Then he disappeared behind the blackened and splintered wall.

Maurice sighed, picked up his rifle and slogged back to the hole he had dug. There was an inch of water in the bottom. He found a log on the ground, pulled it close to the hole and sat on it, looking southwest to where the Germans supposedly were. Taras and Olesh had spread straw on the bottoms of their foxholes to try to make a barrier against the water, but it gradually soaked through. "This damned drizzle just won't let up," Taras moaned as he lit a cigarette.

Maurice put some straw into his own hole as Old Stepan came to the fourth hole, sighed and settled into the water without bothering to put any straw into it, as if he were too resigned to suffering to bother alleviating it even a little.

Maurice peered into the grey, damp night. The only sounds were the slow, soggy wind rattling the dead branches on the trees and the occasional shifting of his fellow sentries. There weren't even any insects at this time of year, no owls or other night creatures.

He shifted to stay awake, pressed his rifle butt against his shoulder, took deep breaths and shook his head when he felt his eyelids closing.

The night dragged on and the four men got wetter and wetter until their relief came, two hours later. Stepan went to find a corner of the barn to sleep in. Maurice, Serhiy Koval and Young Olesh made a tent of their greatcoats, their rifles forming the posts, and lay down for a few hours of fitful sleep. Every hour, they would rotate their positions, so each one had at least some time in the warmest place, between the other two.

Morning came bright and cold. Maurice chafed his arm, which had been on the outside of the trio of sleepers for the last shift of the night.

The quartermaster's men were distributing breakfast, tea and bread. Maurice pulled on his coat, watching a teenaged private carrying a big jug across what had been a farmer's field. He heard the shot a split second after he saw the back of the boy's head explode. Maurice hit the ground before the poor teenager's body did.

The air filled with the chatter of gunfire. An explosion showered mud and twigs on him and bullets ripped holes in the side of the truck near the barn.

Soviet machine guns chattered back. Maurice lifted his head enough to see men scrambling and falling. More shells hit, one blowing the ruined barn to splinters. Someone screamed as the walls fell.

Borys and Mykhailo loaded and fired the Maxim. Maurice crawled on his belly to the berm. A man sprawled over it. An explosion had crushed the side of his head, but Maurice could still recognize Evhen, the scared student from Kalush. The body still clutched the Shpagin submachine gun. Maurice pulled it from the body's grasp and pointed it southwest, in the same direction that Borys was firing the heavy gun.

That was when he saw the Germans. Small groups of men, dashing from cover to cover: trees, mounds and holes in the ground, rocks. In the middle, two tanks headed straight at him, full speed, machine guns firing continuously. Soldiers clung to the deck behind the turrets, each armed with a submachine gun. Behind them were two self-propelled field guns, their crews loading, aiming and firing smoothly and efficiently. The shells burst in the camp every few seconds.

Maurice fired at the men riding the closer tank, but billowing smoke prevented him from seeing whether he hit anything.

Maurice could hear shouting in Russian behind him and all at once men lined the berm, firing rifles over it. From behind him, Maurice heard the whoosh of a mortar, and an explosion burst in the midst of a group of German soldiers.

Then a shell hit directly on the machine gun. Borys and Young Olesh vanished in smoke, dust and flame. The rifleman beside Maurice jerked back and fell, but Maurice was too busy firing Evhen's submachine gun into the smoke to see who it was.

More shouting and a deep boom from behind, and the lead Panzer seemed to skip sideways. Flames leapt up, followed by smoke and its treads stopped. The soldiers riding on it fell or jumped off, and then were cut down by bullets.

Still, the Germans kept coming. A shell hit the front of the berm and a metre of its length collapsed, killing three men. Maurice kept firing in bursts and watched men in grey uniforms fall.

Maurice fired the submachine in spurts until it jammed. He threw it down and picked up his own rifle, aiming and firing as fast as he could.

He heard a growling roar, and from beyond the barn emerged two Soviet tanks, T-34s, both firing their cannons. One hit the second Panzer and almost simultaneously the other hit one of the German self-propelled cannons.

"Keep firing! Kill the bastards!" someone yelled, in Russian. It was Lieutenant Vasilyev, standing amidst the shredded bodies of Borys and Olesh. He brandished his gun and screamed at his men. "With me, men! For Russia!" A shell hit a few metres away and the explosion tore his right arm off above the elbow. Vasilyev fell, screaming and clutching his shoulder with his remaining hand.

A T-34 blasted the second German cannon, and the few soldiers remaining on the field turned and ran. A commissar behind Maurice leapt over the fallen lieutenant, calling the troop to charge. Six men climbed onto the back of one of the tanks, which roared after the retreating Germans.

"Bury, Ivanyuk, Chorny, come on boys," said Sergeant Nikolaev, running over the berm with a submachine gun in his hands. The other men followed, and Maurice wondered whether the other four men in his odalenye were still alive. But he didn't have time to think about it as he followed the sergeant to the other T-34. The others helped him climb onto the deck as the tank roared across the burned fields.

He looked left, then right and saw more T-34s moving with them, followed by groups of soldiers running from cover to cover, using the tanks themselves, the occasional trees, small rises in the ground. They dropped to the ground and fired single shots, got up and moved forward.

Once again, Maurice was astounded by the size of the Red Army. As far as he could see in either direction: tanks, men, guns, horses. Smoke rose, thinning into the bright blue sky. The noise of the engines, the gunfire, the exploding shells made it impossible to think about anything but attacking their attackers.

The tank he rode on followed the other by a few metres. They passed through an opening in another tree windbreak and over a rise, and then they saw they had forced themselves into a trap.

An explosion rocked the front tank in the same moment that Maurice saw more German field guns, the dreaded Stug tank destroyers and an Elefant a hundred metres to their left, between an abandoned farmhouse and another ruined barn, perfectly placed to hit the Soviet tanks on their more vulnerable flanks as they crested the ridge. The T-34 lurched to the right, its turret knocked out of place. Flame and smoke rose from a hole in the side plating.

The German guns opened up. A shell hit Maurice's tank, but the sloping armour deflected it. It flew off and exploded almost harmlessly, but the force threw Maurice from the tank. He hit the ground face down, ashy soil filling his mouth and nose.

Maurice lay as flat as he could on the ground, not moving even though his rifle dug into his chest. He craned his head up to see ahead, still trying not to present any profile that a bullet could hit.

Shells pounded without pause. Ahead, the tank rolled on, its cannon firing, but there were no men riding on it anymore. *Where is Sergeant Nikolaev?* Maurice crawled on his belly back up the slope, his ears aching from the force of the explosion that had knocked him off the tank. The smell of soil, ash and smoke filled his nostrils.

He reached the crest of the low ridge again, rolled behind it and turned around. He could see other Soviet soldiers hunkering down, taking cover where they could. He could not see any German soldiers. Then he saw another ruined farm behind the line of cannons. *They're hiding in there.*

A screaming buzz cut through the din. Maurice and all the other Red soldiers looked up and dismayed at the sight of German planes, flashing silver in the blue sky. They dove on the Red Army, strafing parallel lines of torn soil and bodies, dropping bombs on the tanks. Maurice saw one plane burst into black smoke and veer into the ground behind the Germans' line, and then he had to hide his face as another explosion tore into the Soviet line.

The Red Army halted, bracing itself against the Germans' savage counterattack to retake Latvia.

The shelling slowed and halted, replaced by the whirring chatter of the high-speed German heavy machine guns. Maurice tried to press himself into the soil. There was no use trying to shoot back—that would just give away his position.

With one cheek on the ground, he could just see the Red Army executing its classic move: overwhelming the enemy with massive force. A line of T-34s advanced, firing machine guns almost continuously and their cannons as fast as the gunners could load them. Men rode behind the turrets, firing rifles and submachine guns, and others advanced between and behind them, finding cover where they could, falling to German fire when they couldn't.

There were Soviet planes in the air now, banking and turning like angry hawks, three to every German plane. Nothing could withstand the flood of the Red Army, pressing its way down the shallow slope.

A tank shell hit one of the German cannons, and a Red Army plane took out another's crew. So many shells were exploding, Maurice could hardly see the field anymore for all the soil, ash and smoke in the air.

The German self-propelled guns began to withdraw, and the ground troops began taking rear-guard action, firing to protect the guns. When he saw a German machine gun crew running, pulling their gun behind them, he raised himself and his borrowed gun. He aimed at two Germans who were firing their own submachine guns toward the advancing Red Army. He felt a little spasm of satisfaction when one fell sideways, knocking his companion down, and then he hit the dirt again before he drew fire himself.

He saw something moving behind the disabled T-34 and slithered closer to it. Black smoke poured from a hole in its turret. As he neared the tank, Maurice could see a Red soldier, covered in mud, waving him to come closer.

It was Sergeant Nikolaev. A trickle of blood has cleared a path through the dirt on his face, from above his left eye to his jaw. But his hazel eyes were clear and determined.

"Sergeant? Are you hurt?" Maurice asked.

Nikolaev shook his head. "Come with me, Bury. There's a nest of them over there, just ahead of the other tank." He turned and crawled around the dead tank, and Maurice wondered for a second about its crew. But then he had to follow his sergeant, flattening himself on the ground again to look beyond it.

His mouth fell open when he saw the remainder of his odalenye sheltering behind the tank: the corporal Ostap Shewchuk, Taras Kuchnir, Old Stepan Chorny, Mykhailo Boyko, Serhi Koval and Oleh Vohk. *Evhen, Borys, young Olesh, dead, three from our unit lost within minutes. And the lieutenant—is he alive or dead? Did he bleed out?*

The sergeant interrupted his stream of thought. "We're going to get to those bushes over there," he waved at a small stand of dead trees fifty metres ahead of the tank. "We'll use the trees as cover to that shed over there, and from there we'll be able to fire on the trench Fritz is using in front of the farm."

"We'll never make it," Maurice said.

Nikolaev turned on him like an angry dog. "Don't question my orders, you kokhol coward," he snarled.

"It's not cowardice, Sergeant." Maurice pointed to the left. "There's another trench fifty or sixty metres that way, to cut off any retreat. They'll shoot us all from the flank if we run across fifty metres of open ground."

Nikolaev crouched and peered around the rear corner of the tank to where Maurice was pointing. Sixty metres away, between the farm and the windbreak, was another trench he hadn't seen. He could count at least eight flared German helmets above the lip, which seemed to be watching the action between the dueling T-34s and Panzers.

"Right. Okay, boys, that's our target. Fix bayonets and we'll rush it on my count."

Maurice felt cold in his bowels. Bayonets meant up-close fighting. But there was no time to think, no time to react other than to follow the other boys in fixing the long bayonet to the barrel of his rifle.

The Red Army was advancing and the Germans fleeing, but the men in the trench were covering their retreat with flanking fire. They concentrated on the men riding on the tanks, now ahead of Maurice's group and to their left.

Sergeant Nikolaev crouched at the back corner of the tank, intent on the trench. He held up one hand. "One, two …" When the Germans seemed to be focused away from them, he sprang to his feet without finishing the count. He ran toward the trench.

The men jumped after him, running flat out. Maurice could only hope one of his own men wouldn't stab him accidentally, and they closed the fifty metres to the trench before one of the German soldiers turned toward them.

Nikolaev shot him immediately with a short burst from his Shpagin, then leaped over the trench. Shewchuk and Kuchnir leapt over the edge, impaling Germans before they had a chance to scream.

Maurice stepped on the lip of the trench and paused. It was enough for the grey-uniformed private below him to grab the barrel of his rifle. The stock smashed into Maurice's face and his mouth filled with blood. His vision swam, but he held tighter to the rifle. He looked at the German soldier and thrust his rifle forward and down.

The bayonet penetrated the German's throat as easily as if it were made of bread. He looked up, blood spurting bright red from his neck and his mouth. Then Maurice made a mistake. He looked down into his victim's eyes and saw them fade from bright blue to dull grey.

Maurice yanked the bayonet out of the body. It toppled onto the bottom of the trench, its helmet falling to reveal cropped blond hair. He could not have even been twenty years old.

Maurice felt something solid in his mouth and spat it out, and only then realized three of his front teeth were now lying in his own blood on the ground.

Nikolaev crouched on the far side of the trench and fired single shots with his submachine gun, making certain the German men were dead. He jumped down into the trench, and his men followed, trampling and stumbling over the bodies.

"Get down, Maurice!" someone said, and Taras Kuchnir pulled him into the trench. He landed on the body he had just killed.

Maurice began to tremble. He closed his eyes, only to see the German soldier's eyes fade again. He fell to his knees and vomited onto some body, splattering his knees.

No one else seemed to care. The fighting was nearly over. The German tank destroyers and Panzers burned on the fields. The farmhouse burned, too, and a T-34 had driven over the barn, knocking it into splinters. Bodies lay everywhere, German and Soviet. Farther off, the Soviet tanks kept going, chasing down Germans, their machine guns and the men riding on the rear decks firing occasionally.

It was less than two hours since Maurice had woken up, and he had lost his front teeth, a third of his unit were dead, his commander was maimed, who knew how many more young Russians and Ukrainians killed, how many Germans.

He spat blood out again and ran his teeth against his aching gums. His mouth felt so strange, now.

Mykhailo gave him a dirty kerchief, and he dabbed at his mouth. "Put it in your mouth to soak up the blood. Bite down as hard as you can bear," said Corporal Shewchuk. "We can't afford to have you bleed out from a lost tooth."

Maurice tried to reply, but his jaw hurt too much. He gingerly pushed the kerchief into his mouth, just a little, and closed his jaws as much as he could stand.

Even though he knew he had been lucky to have lost only teeth, some part of him mourned them. He did not allow himself to mourn Evhen, Borys or Young Olesh.

Not yet. Not until this is over. I won't survive if I weep while I should be fighting.

Into Lithuania

July 1944

The regiment had lost so many men to the German counter-strike that they had to reorganize the companies. Captain Baranov merged Lieutenant Vasilyev's odalenye into one that had lost most of its men, but not its commander, nor its Maxim machine gun.

Lieutenant Maxim Schwatchko looked like he had been an athlete before the war: tall and fit with massive shoulders and arms. He had thick, black hair that swept over his forehead and angry brown eyes. He commanded with terse orders, as if he were about to hit anyone who questioned him.

There were three privates left alive in his odalenye, all Russian, all just twenty years old. Vadim Glukhov was thin with brown hair and large, expressive eyes.

Grigory Kornev was the newest recruit, sent from a farm near the Latvian border that had been razed by the retreating Germans. He stood very straight all the time, as if he were trying to emulate the soldiers in the posters. "Fucking Germans killed my whole family," he said in response to "I'm Maurice Bury."

Dmitry Rusnak always looked sleepy. Short and stocky, he had dark hair and his face always bore a trace of stubble, even after he shaved. He was chatty, and somehow found optimism, even when the bullets flew.

The deep penetration strategy was so effective, the Red Army's advance so fast, that the supply lines had trouble keeping up.

One night, the sentries woke the men in the unit at midnight. Captain Baranov led the company away from the main body of the army. They marched along a muddy road, stopping at a deserted farm. Maurice knew they were somewhere in Lithuania, but he had given up on asking exactly where they were—Lieutenant Schwatchko either would not tell him or didn't know.

A soldier busted the farmhouse door in with the butt of his rifle. Captain Baranov, Commissar Sorkin and the lieutenants, including Schwatchko, went inside to discuss plans, but mostly to look for any valuables or liquor left behind.

Schwatchko came out a few minutes later. "Sergeant Nikolaev, set up sentries along that raised bank over there," he growled, pointing to a small ridge that the farmer had probably once used as a road for wagons, raised above the fields that would be soft mud in a wet season.

"What about the other side? Fritz could come from there, too," said the Sergeant.

"Don't question my orders, Sergeant," Lieutenant Schwatchko said. "But for your information, Orlov's *odalenye* is looking south and Federov's is guarding the west. Now get the men into position."

Nikolaev saluted, more formally than usual, Maurice thought. The sergeant turned to him. "Bury, Kuchnir and Koval, set up the Maxim on that bank." He turned to Old Stepan. "Grampa, you make sure they have plenty of ammunition. The rest of you, find someplace to take cover. The action begins at sunrise, unless something happens in the meantime." Maurice did not want to think about what "something happens" could be.

Setting up the heavy, clumsy machine gun in the dark was especially challenging. The wheels kept getting stuck in ruts and holes in the churned, muddy ground. By the time they had it pointed over the raised bank and settled firmly on the ground, Maurice estimated it was close to 4 a.m.

He leaned against the grassy bank, the smell of damp earth in his nostrils, laying the barrel of his rifle across the top and looking forward. He dozed off, waking as the sky to the east, behind him, was just starting to turn grey.

He straightened and stretched. Around him, other men dozed against the bank, too. Behind them, he could see a shadowed figure standing straight, looking at the Red Army soldiers. From his posture, it had to be Commissar Sorkin.

Sergeant Nikolai Nikolaev was on the other side of Mykhailo, alert, scanning the darker shadows to the west.

Slowly, the dawn illuminated the landscape in front of them, to the west. At the moment orange light tinted a cloud in the east, Maurice heard a deep *boom* to the south.

Mykhailo jumped alert, eyes wide. He clutched his rifle to his chest and looked left and right.

Another *boom,* followed by a continuous drumming that they felt in the ground as much as they heard. Now, all the men along the earthen bank were wide awake, looking south.

"It's started, boys," said Sergeant Nikolaev. One hand slid down and up the barrel of his submachine gun in a loving gesture. A smile played at the corners of his mouth.

As the sun rose, Maurice could see a line of trees that formed a windbreak about fifty metres away in front of them. Beyond the line, the land sloped gently upward to a crest.

"You think Fritz is under those trees?" asked Dmitry Rusnak, on Maurice's right.

"Fritz is everywhere," Maurice said. "If it's not the Germans, it's partisans. Not everyone loves the Russians."

"What do you mean? We're liberating Lithuania from the Nazis," Dmitry said.

Lieutenant Schwatchko appeared between them at that moment, throwing himself chest-down against the earthen bank. The pace of the artillery fire accelerated, a continuous drumming that made the grass on the bank vibrate in time with the soles of Maurice's feet.

"This is it, boys. The main group is driving Fritz this way. They're going to come through that gap over there," Schwatchko said, pointing at a gap in the windbreak that was just wide enough for a single tank to come through. "When they do, cut them down. Every single one of the bastards. No survivors, no prisoners. Got it?"

"Yes, sir!" said Mykhailo.

"Fucking Germans killed my whole family and burned down my house," Grigory Kornev said again, already aiming his rifle.

"Don't chamber a round yet, private," Sergeant Nikolaev said. "There's no sense endangering your comrades unnecessarily.

But Lieutenant Schwatchko slapped Kornev on the back. "That's the spirit. Be ready to kill, private." He disappeared, running down the line of men.

The drumming continued for an hour, then suddenly ended. Maurice heard a low, buzzing drone and turned to look over his shoulder to see a row of Pe-2s, the Soviets' light bombers, flying low. Maurice could not see where they dove beyond the trees, but he felt the impacts of their bombs in the ground beneath his feet, and in his hands, too, when they braced against the earthen bank.

Overhead, the men could see the silvery flash of Messerschmidt fighters like fish fighting the hook. Soviet fighters buzzed from the east, the sun at their backs in an aerial dance of death.

Even though all the Red Army soldiers were lying in protected positions, waiting for the enemy, the first appearance of a grey uniform between the trees shocked every one of them. Maurice had to will his hands to loosen on the stock of his rifle when he saw one man in a *Wehrmacht* uniform appear over the crest of the low hill in front of him.

"Hold your fire," said Sergeant Nikolaev. "Wait till we see more of them and they can't get away."

The single man on the slope was soon joined by another, then a whole company. They ran down the hill the way only men pursued by a deadly, irresistible force will run.

A single Panzer appeared in the gap, with two men riding on it. Then another tank, and more men in grey uniforms and flared helmets.

"Now," said Sergeant Nikolaev. He squeezed the trigger of his black PPS-43 submachine gun and cut down the first man, who fell into the grass, arms and legs loose as a rag doll.

The other Germans dropped to the ground, firing their submachine guns. Maurice heard the Maxim rattling to his right and saw German soldiers falling like the wheat they walked through.

The lead Panther tank opened up with its machine guns. Maurice and all the others in his company dropped below the lip of the bank as bullets zipped over their heads.

Maurice raised his head over the edge of the earthen bank. To his left, a heavy 100 mm anti-tank gun opened up. A round hit the Panzer, penetrating the armour. Maurice saw the tank shake. The top hatch popped open and flame and smoke poured out of it.

More Germans poured over the hill, running from the unstoppable Soviet force behind them. Fire from behind the earth bank cut them down.

Maurice looked to his left. Sergeant Nikolaev fired single rounds or short bursts. Every shot brought down a German soldier.

On Maurice's right, the Maxim machine gun rattled continuously. Serhiy Koval fed the ammunition belt into the side of the gun as Taras Kuchnir held the trigger. Occasionally, he hit something. Sparks flew off the side of the crippled Panzer. A German soldier rose to fire back. Taras pumped six high-calibre rounds into him.

Maurice aimed his rifle carefully at the German soldiers in the vanguard, knowing they posed the greatest threat to his comrades. He got a grey uniform in the sights of his gun and squeezed the trigger. The man fell backward, disappearing in the tall grass.

The remaining Panzer fired its cannon toward the earthen bank. The round struck twenty metres to Maurice's left. The explosion sent soil high into the air, and buried the comrades sheltering behind it.

The Panzer's machine gun strafed left. Sergeant Nikolaev, Mykhailo, Maurice and Dmitry ducked below the edge. Nikolaev popped up again a moment later, firing his submachine gun.

To the right, the heavy anti-tank gun spoke again. Flames enveloped the Panzer.

But now there were a hundred German soldiers only fifty metres from the earthen bank.

"Get them! Everyone shoot!" Sergeant Nikolaev shouted, laying down a continuous stream of bullets from his submachine gun. Rows of Germans fell into the high grass, but they kept coming. The Germans had fast, efficient submachine guns that sprayed the bank and the men above it. Maurice saw a man to his right fly back as a bullet hit him.

He dropped below the lip along with Mykhailo. He waited a beat, then rose again to shoot.

Mykhailo stayed down, shaking. Nikolaev grabbed him by his jacket and pulled him upright with one hand. "Fight, you kokhol coward."

Maurice fired at a German soldier and ducked down again to pull back the bolt on his rifle. He popped up again, aimed and fired, then dropped below the bank without waiting to see whether he had hit anything as he chambered another round. Wide-eyed, Mykhailo copied Maurice's action, firing over the bank then dropping down immediately to chamber another round.

Nikolaev stayed where he was, coolly firing single shots or short bursts from his submachine gun—along with other Red Army soldiers strung out for fifty metres along the berm.

As Maurice loaded a fresh magazine into his rifle, an explosion shook the bank. He closed his eyes for a moment. The noise, the smell of cordite and smoke and oil, urine, the earth under his nose, the vibration of the earth under his body— took his mind back to the bank of the Psel River three years earlier, when he had been a lieutenant commanding an anti-tank unit. He remembered the Panzer splashing across the shallow river, unstoppable, merciless, immune to the fire of the panicking Red Army. He remembered seeing whole squadrons of Soviet soldiers blown to bits by the German cannons, entire armies surrounded and cut to shreds.

Another explosion shook the ground behind his back, covering him in soil. When he opened his eyes again, he was surprised to see a rifle in his hands, instead of an officer's revolver, and cloth boots instead of black leather on his feet.

I'm not an officer anymore. It's not 1941. It's 1944, and we're not retreating, we're driving the Germans back to Germany.

We're winning.

He pushed the full magazine home and rose, putting the barrel of his rifle on the top of the bank. The battle was nearly over. One Panzer burned, surrounded by dead bodies in grey uniforms. The second tank still fired a machine gun, but one tread had been blown off and it leaned onto that side. Maurice saw the turret swivel toward him and heard the anti-tank gun to his right. The Panzer shook and exploded. All the men ducked below the top of the bank.

Except for Sergeant Nikolaev. He stayed in position, firing his submachine gun in short, controlled bursts. "Get back up and finish them off, you fucking cowards," he growled.

Maurice, Dmitry and Mykhailo rose to see both Panzers burning. Dead men lay across the field. A German officer rose from the wheat and ran back toward the tree line, even though they could all hear more explosions and gunfire from behind the hill.

Dmitry fired and the German fell. "Got him."

As Maurice turned to Dmitry, he heard a metallic *clink* at the same moment a small, round hole appeared in the side of Dmitry's helmet. The young man toppled into Maurice's arms, blood streaming over his face.

"Son of a bitch," said Nikolaev, firing a long burst over the bank.

Maurice laid Dmitry's body gently on the ground at his feet. "Get up, Bury," he heard the sergeant say. "Get up and shoot."

Maurice rose just high enough to see over the bank. The flames on the Panzer were the only things to move on the field.

Lieutenant Schwatchko climbed onto the bank and jumped onto the field, his heavy revolver in his hand. He walked to a body in the wheat, and Maurice could see the man was struggling to rise. Schwatchko bent and pulled the wounded man up by the shoulder of his uniform. He turned toward the Soviets. "This is the bastard who shot comrade Rusnak." He raised his revolver and fired into the German's bare head, letting the body drop.

Mykhailo turned and vomited at Maurice's feet.

Niemen River

October 10, 1944

The sun shone into Maurice's eyes as Sergeant Nikolaev called a halt. He leaned back and let his pack slide off his shoulders, then sat down, grateful for a minute's rest. The temperature had been dropping all day, and Maurice's nerves were pulled taut from the sounds of machine guns and bombs that grew ever closer as they marched. The Germans continued to retreat, but the men knew they were marching toward an enemy defensive position.

The flatland of Lithuania continued as far as they could see, but maybe two hundred metres to the south, a shallow, broad river valley crossed the plain. That was the source of occasional gun- and cannon-fire.

"The Niemen. Across that is East Prussia. Germany," said a young officer, passing by. "Don't get too comfortable. That's where we're heading."

By sunset, the gunfire died down. The two armies were stalemated, facing each other across the valley of the Niemen River, also known as the Neman and, in local Lithuanian, the Nemunas. When the sky was dark, the officers quietly ordered the men in Maurice's troop to move to the fortifications the Red Army had already dug, fifty metres from the bank.

No one knew, no one told them, but Stavka, the Soviet high command, had already tried to penetrate into East Prussia to take the strategic fortress of Konigsberg. The Baltic Offensive had succeeded in driving the Germans out of most of Estonia and Latvia and had finally taken Riga back from the Germans. Soviet General Bagramyan had pushed the Third Panzer Army down the Baltic coast, where they holed up in the town of Klaipeda, which the Germans had renamed Memel in 1939.

With the town surrounded, the Soviets then committed four armies to attack into East Prussia, driving for a line fifty kilometres further south.

General Erhard Raus's Third Panzer Army stopped the Red Army, though, and held it at the Neman River. The Stavka decided to hold that position until it could bring in more reinforcements to allow it to use its deep operations strategy. Maurice's unit was part of that.

The soldiers already at the river had dug trenches and made fortifications a few metres back from the banks. Maurice's unit found a place to set up camp. The next morning, they settled into a new routine: patrolling the fortifications, watching the enemy across the broad river, firing a few shots across just to let the enemy know they were watching. When their watch was over, they went back for food and snatched what sleep they could.

At night, Maurice did not sleep much. He knew he should have made the most of this break in the fighting, but he couldn't relax. *Something big is going to happen soon.*

One day near the end of October, the officers seemed to be stirring more than usual. In the evening, as the sun hit the horizon, the major called the junior officers into a circle; then the lieutenant of Maurice's new odalenye, Mikhailov, gathered the men. "We're going to do some reconnaissance across the river," he said. He was short, broad, with large brown eyes, thick eyebrows and thick, dark brown hair. "Find out where Fritz has his cannons, tanks, and most important, supplies. Get the directions back to our gunners.

You'll have to be smart, quiet, and you can't lose your head, or we're all done for. The Major's looking for four men."

Sergeant Nikolaev was a tough communist who acted older than his years. He stepped in front of the unit. "Okay, with me, it will be Oleh, Maurice and Mykhailo—it's your turn, comrades." Maurice suddenly felt as though his guts were wide, hollow and empty at the sound of his name. Numbly he followed the sergeant and the other boys to the quartermaster's wagon. He felt another cold shock when he saw German uniforms lying on the ground.

"Get dressed, boys," said the quartermaster, leering.

Grumbling, they stripped off their Red Army uniforms and struggled into the tight-fitting *Wehrmacht* clothes. They griped as they swapped tunics and pants until each had as close a fit as they could manage.

Maurice picked one up: a corporal's uniform, dirty and torn. There was a dark smudge along the pant leg; in the twilight, he couldn't tell if it was oil or blood. As he pulled on the tunic, he couldn't help but squirm thinking that its previous owner had died wearing it.

"Hey, Maurice, you got a promotion!" Mykhailo laughed.

"Shut up," said Lieutenant Mikhailov, and handed out German small arms: handguns, extra ammunition clips to Sergeant Nikolaev, who was now wearing an *unterleutnant*'s uniform. Then he gave each of them a tiny flashlight. "Use these to signal us when you find the targets," he instructed.

They walked silently to the riverbank, staying low so they wouldn't be silhouetted against the purple sky for the German machine gunners across the river.

"Keep quiet, boys, and stay low. Crawl on your bellies. Don't do anything to let the Germans see you, because if you do, we're dead," Nikolaev said. Without another word, he led them slowly down the bank to the river's edge, where a private held the rope of a tiny wooden boat. He looked uncomfortable at the sight of men in German uniforms approaching from the eastern bank, but he relaxed when the Sergeant winked.

Maurice climbed aboard with the others, and the private pushed off before climbing smoothly into the boat. He was an expert boatman, rowing without splashing, barely making a ripple. Even so, Maurice felt sure that the Germans could hear every bump and creak. He expected the revving sound of a German machine gun any second, expected to feel bullets tear into him. But nothing came, except the sounds of the night, the water lapping on the side of the boat, and stressed breathing of the men on it.

As the far shore approached, he felt fear grow even stronger. He felt like he was going to be sick, but forced it down. *I've faced danger before. I've come through. I may die tonight, but I won't run.* He hefted the German pistol. It felt strangely comforting, and he realized it was the first time he had held a handgun since his days in UPA. He thought, also, of his time as a Red Army officer. It felt so long ago.

They finally reached the south bank, which was a little steeper than the north side. They tried to climb out without making noise, but silence was impossible. As they splashed in the water a machine gun at the top of the bank roared out. Bullets whipped overhead, raising a deadly row of pinpoint splashes in the river behind them.

All four men threw themselves forward, pressing their bellies into the muddy bank. The machine gun raked back and forth, back and forth, and Maurice imagined the water splashing up in lines. He felt drops hitting his back. He did not dare breathe.

The firing stopped, only to start again after a few seconds. When it stopped again, Maurice realized that the German sentries had only heard them, but hadn't seen four men splash onto the riverbank. *Their fortifications are back from the bank*, he realized, *like ours are. They can't see us, but we can't see them, either.* Maurice knew he did not dare move, not even to raise his head.

"Stay down, boys," the sergeant said softly, but that just brought another sustained burst of machine gun fire from the top of the bank. No one said another word.

Maurice tried again to flatten himself into the ground. Overhead, he could barely make out the edge where the Lithuanian plain fell into the river's valley.

Suddenly, for no reason the four men could see, furious fighting began overhead. The Germans started firing what seemed like thousands of shells across the river. The Soviets answered with heavy machine guns, rattling. The four would-be spies heard explosions over them and knew their comrades were firing mortars. A whoosh meant that Katyusha rockets were streaking across the river. All the men clinging to the bank knew that whether they were hit by errant shells from German or Soviet guns was only a matter of luck.

Gradually, the fighting died down again to sporadic bursts from machine guns, just a few shots to keep the enemy at bay. All five men on the south bank, the four would-be scouts and the boatman, knew that moving meant bullets for them, so they stayed still, feet freezing in the water.

Maurice soon began to shiver. He felt so tired, but knew there was no possibility of sleeping. Sometimes he closed his eyes, only to see nightmare visions of the Panzer crossing the Poltava, Messerschmidts over Kyiv. Every few minutes, guns fired from one side of the river, and were answered from the other: *rrr-rrr* from the Germans, *rat-tat-tat-tat-tat* from the Soviets.

"*Maurice,*" someone whispered hoarsely from his right. Mykhailo. Carefully, Maurice turned his head without raising it off the ground. "I have to take a piss."

"So what do you want me to do about it?" he whispered back. He could almost see the fool, pushed up on his shoulders, trembling.

RRR-RRR! roared the German gun overhead. Across the river, the Soviets answered, *rat-tat-tat-tat*. Mykhailo threw himself down and was quiet, but Maurice could see his shoulders shaking.

Maurice felt now that he, too, had to pee. Damn Mykhailo! If he hadn't mentioned it, Maurice might not have thought about peeing for another hour or so. Too late now. He tried to think about something else, and realized that his boots had soaked through and were now filled with water over his ankles.

If it's not one misery, it's another.

The night wore on. The shooting stopped for a long time, well over an hour, Maurice thought. Then, from his right, he heard Mykhailo whispering again, but more softly. "Oh, hell, I've pissed myself."

Finally, dawn greyed the limited landscape that Maurice could see. Shivering, Maurice was grateful for the coming day that might warm him, at least a little, but at the same time wished for the dark that had so far hidden him from the Germans.

As the sun's first rays spread over the battleground, gunners on both sides of the river took the opportunity to at least pretend to aim. The firing started again, and gradually died down. Maurice knew then that they were still out of sight of the German gunners, but at the same time, they couldn't go back, for moving away from the sloping bank brought them into the gunner's field of vision.

The four men waited, shivering against the banks of the river. By mid-morning, Maurice realized he felt emptiness in his belly and pressure on his bladder. By noon, shivering under a weak November sun behind grey clouds, all four had wet themselves.

In mid-afternoon, Maurice reached carefully into his jacket pocket and brought out the only rations he had: a small bar of chocolate, courtesy of the Americans. Careful not to raise his head, he unwrapped one end of the Hershey bar and took a small bite. It did absolutely nothing to satisfy his hunger, so he tried his best to eat only a few bites at a time. All too soon, the whole bar was gone.

When the sun finally set, the men were shivering uncontrollably. Sergeant Nikolaev squirmed around until he was facing across the river toward the Soviet-held side. He waited longer, until the sky was completely black. The clouds covered the moon; there was almost absolute darkness. Nikolayev reached out and touched the other three on the shoulders and nodded toward the boat.

This time, they were especially careful not to make a sound. Expecting to feel bullets ripping through him any second, Maurice did not hear even a drop of water fall into the river as he raised his soaking boots over the gunwale. He put his feet down so slowly they made no sound, then sat silently.

It seemed to take hours for each man to climb aboard without making noise, but they did it. The boatman rowed, silently again, and the other four crouched low. Finally, they reached the north bank. Maurice felt both relief and misgiving. *We didn't see the German side. We failed to bring in the intelligence. The major won't be happy.* He could hear the Commissar screaming at them for treasonous incompetence.

But the major seemed genuinely happy and relieved when the Sergeant Nikolaev, still in his wet, muddy German uniform, saluted smartly. "All here, all accounted for, *tovarisch* Major."

"Change into dry clothes and reassemble in ten minutes, Sergeant," the Major replied.

This is it, Maurice thought. *We're going to be shot.*

Instead, the Major had a handful of medals. "For bravery," he said as he pinned the medals to each of the five soldiers' chests and then kissed each one on both cheeks. "I know you don't think that you achieved your objective, but the fire you drew showed our gunners where their guns are. We're re-aiming for the big push tomorrow morning."

Even though it was already late, the Major sent them to the mess tent for a special meal, with extra meat and bread and a bottle of Russian brandy. The celebration did not last long, but the five of them savoured it.

The next morning, Maurice was back in his trench, looking down his rifle's barrel and waiting for the order to charge across the river.

Germany

October 1944

After Operation Bagration drove the Germans out of Belorussia, Lithuania and much of Poland by the autumn of 1944, the Germans launched two counter-operations in Lithuania. Doppelkopf and Casar managed to hold the Soviets back and preserve a link between the two major German forces, Army Group North and Army Group Centre along the Baltic Coast.

On October 5, Soviet General Bagramyan launched the Memel Offensive, again employing the Soviet deep penetration strategy. Attacking along a 100-kilometre front, the Red Army broke through on the first day and drove 16 kilometres northwest toward the Baltic coast. The entire 5th Guards Tank Army drove into the breach. In two days, the Reds reached the sea, severing the two Germany army groups.

Nearly 200,000 German troops, 33 divisions, withdrew to the Courland Pocket, an area around the Baltic city of Memel, now the Lithuanian city of Klaipeda. The city is on a body of water called the Curonian Lagoon, which is separated from the Baltic Sea by a narrow spit of land that extends from the East Prussian territory of Koenigsberg northeast toward Memel.

Meanwhile, in August, the people of Warsaw rose up against the German occupation, counting on the support of the Red Army which was less than twenty miles away. But Stalin ordered the army not to help the Poles. Instead, the USSR let the Germans consume precious resources putting down the Warsaw Uprising, counting on the two sides to weaken each other.

The Courland Pocket held out against the Soviets until the end of the war, not surrendering until two days after Hitler's death. The Soviets attacked the Pocket again and again, losing thousands of men, aircraft and tanks and gaining only a few kilometres of territory.

Courland was a valiant but futile effort. In January 1945, with Army Group Courland effectively pinned down, the Red Army built up a five-to-one superiority in men and materiél over the Germans. They bypassed Courland and Memel, drivinAg hundreds of kilometres west in just two weeks.

After months of inaction on the banks of the Niemen, Maurice and the others in his odalenye were shocked to realize one morning that the enemy had withdrawn.

The orders came down from the commissars to the officers, and then to the men: they were about to cross the Niemen.

Into Königsberg. East Prussia.

Germany.

The shock troops using the deep operations strategy had done their work, pouring across East Prussia, sweeping the German army through the snow of early 1945. German civilians went with them, except for a few, stubborn or unlucky enough to face the Reds.

Maurice's company entered a small town in Koenigsburg, remarkably intact for a city in a war zone. Maurice and his odalenye walked along a road, three men pulling the Maxim gun, the rest holding their rifles across their chests, ready to fire.

Commissar Sorkin came up, his uniform perfectly clean and pressed. *How the hell did he manage that in the snow and mud?* Sorkin called the men together. "Remember this, comrades: we're now in enemy territory. We are no longer liberating occupied countries. Every civilian you see is your enemy. Never forget that, and never let your guard down. Remember how the Germans starved our brothers in Leningrad. Remember how they burned down our homes, destroyed our cities, enslaved our people, raped our women." He paused and looked each man in the eyes. "No mercy."

After four years of occupation, of looting and enslavement, of the rape of their mothers, sisters and daughters, the murder of their fathers and brothers, the men of the USSR took out their revenge on the women and elderly left behind by the Germans.

One unusually warm winter day, as Soviet planes buzzed in a clear blue sky, Maurice's unit followed a group of tanks across the Polish plain. A warm wind and the sunshine turned the snow into soft, almost welcoming cover on the ground, but a black mess behind the tanks' treads.

Maurice's odalenye and several more followed the wake of shock troops that had driven deep into Germany. They passed dead horses and the burning hulks of Panzers. They could see the SS insignia on the collars of the dead men on the fields and in the trenches. *The SS, the fanatics who will never surrender to their last bullet.*

"I heard that Fritz is rushing to surrender to the Americans and the English because they don't want to surrender to us," said Old Stepan, leading the horse that hauled the ammunition wagon.

"I'm not going to take any prisoners," said Serhiy Koval. "Not after they killed Young Olesh. I'm going to kill every fucking German I see."

"Look sharp there," Corporal Shewchuk warned. He pointed ahead and to the right, where a T-34's machine gun fired into a tidy German farm building. Splinters flew but there was no returning fire, and Maurice wondered if the tank gunner was just having fun.

He heard more gunfire and felt a shove. "Down, boys!" Shewchuk shouted. Maurice threw himself to the ground, banging his nose against the butt of his rifle.

More gunfire followed, the zipping buzz of the German heavy machine gun. Behind him, he heard the slower Russian guns answer.

He dared to raise his head just enough to see, about a hundred metres away, a slight rise in the ground. A bunker, he thought. Fritz made a bunker and some SS fanatics have hidden there, waiting for the second echelon to walk into their trap.

Two Red Army soldiers sprinted across the field for the slight shelter of a leafless tree, carrying a mortar between them. The German gun buzzed again and both of them fell, wet snow splashing. Every Soviet rifle and submachine gun opened up, trained on the low opening of the bunker. Two men in Maurice's unit knelt behind the Maxim gun, and sent a stream of bullets toward the bunker.

To no effect. At that range, the Soviet soldiers could not hope to send a bullet into the low, narrow loophole the Germans fired from.

Until another group came from the side, taking advantage of the covering fire. "Hold your fire, boys!" Sergeant Nikolaev called out as two Red Army men tossed grenades inside. Twin explosions blew the earth-and-concrete roof off and smoke rose into the sky.

The Soviets stayed on their bellies, watching the bunker. After several minutes, they saw something moving in the billowing smoke. A dirty cloth that might have once been white waved and a man emerged, holding a hand over his face. Another came behind him, holding the cloth aloft. They both wore the flared helmets of the wehrmacht.

Then someone fired a three-round burst, followed by another. Both the German soldiers fell, and Maurice spun to see Koval behind the shield of the Maxim.

"They were surrendering," said Taras Kuchnir.

"Bastards both still had their guns, didn't they?" Koval retorted. "They were tricking us. I told you, I'm not giving the fucking Germans any mercy."

A group of men approached the remains of the bunker cautiously, their rifles and submachine guns in front of them. They fired a few rounds into the holes in it, just to make sure anyone left inside was dead.

Maurice waited until everyone else in his unit was standing again before rising to his feet. Only then did he realize he had been holding his breath for—how long, he could not say.

They entered a small town along a road whose pavement had been thoroughly chewed up by tank treads and peppered with craters. A small house at the edge of the town smoked, and more smoke rose from what looked to be the central square.

Captain Baranov pointed at another house, this one intact. On the porch stood a middle-aged man in a white shirt, glaring defiantly at the passing Red Army. A corporal led three soldiers through his garden gate and up his steps. "What are you looking at, old man?" Corporal Shewchuk demanded. The resident said nothing, but continued to glare at the passing parade. "Answer me when I talk to you, you Nazi dog," the Corporal yelled.

The homeowner continued to ignore the soldier on his porch until Shewchuk punched him in the face. The man staggered back, but still refused to look at his assailant. The corporal picked up his rifle and smashed the butt into the German's stomach, then pushed him over the railing of his porch. A woman inside the house screamed and opened the front door, but Shewchuk shoved her back inside.

He pointed at his men, who picked the German up and pulled him to the street. He spat blood onto the snow as he stumbled behind the marching soldiers.

His wife opened the door again, calling after him. Corporal Shewchuk smashed his rifle butt into her midsection, sending her to the floor. He walked down the path and caught up with his captive and his men in the parade ahead of Maurice's unit.

Maurice found Commissar Sorkin in the group. He was looking at the corporal and his captive. But he said nothing.

They reached the town's central square. Black smoke poured out of the town hall's windows.

At the corner of the square, a shop's door lay on the ground among the glass shards of its shattered front window. Maurice saw three Red Army soldiers, privates, standing inside as the bare ass of a fourth man rose and fell between the spread legs of a woman on the floor. She didn't even scream, just whimpered. Maurice saw the man on the ground rise, and another got down to take his turn.

Commissar Sorkin looked into the shop, too, and walked faster. "After what the Germans did to us, what can you expect," he said, and walked on.

As the Red Armies moved through East Prussia, Maurice saw the character and behaviour of the "boys" change. Groups of men smashed into large, wealthy homes and took what they wanted, including women.

Political officers put posters on walls and poles that read "Red Army Soldier: You are now on German soil. The hour of revenge has struck!"

Marshal Rossokovsky, head of the First Belorussian Front, signed an order to shoot looters and rapists on the spot. Occasionally, the officers and commissars would enforce the orders. But most of the time, officers not only turned away, but took part themselves.

Historians would later report Stalin responding to critics of the Red Army by asking "Can't he understand it if a soldier who has crossed thousands of kilometres through blood and fire and death has fun with a woman or takes some trifle?"

Maurice walked past, looking straight ahead when another Soviet soldier would beckon him toward a house where others streamed out with treasures, or where he heard the whimpers and cries of young girls as their mothers lay bloodied in the snow.

Keep your head down, Maurice, he told himself over and over. *You're heading west. To Berlin, and if you're still alive when this ends, you'll keep going west until you're back home at last.*

In Montreal, Canada. Not in the USSR.

I am not going back to the USSR.

Approaching Berlin

Prussia, April 1945

An April sun warmed Maurice's chenille as the unit woke from the first real sleep they had had in weeks. Where the war had not blackened the landscape, wild flowers bloomed white and yellow and red in the new, green grass. A gentle wind ruffled his clothes and hair.

Maurice felt uplifted. He felt hope, for the first time in a very long while.

"The war will be over soon, Maurice," said Mykhailo, rolling up his chenille. "Even the Germans know it."

As if to remind them it was not over yet, cannons boomed in the west. "We still have some fighting to do," Maurice replied.

Sergeant Nikolayev strode up, helmet fastened, chenille rolled and tied across his back, submachine gun slung over his shoulder. "Keep your eyes sharp," he said. "Fritz is just waiting for us to get careless."

Junior officers blew whistles, tanks rumbled ahead and the men began walking westward, "mopping up" stray Germans. Soviet planes crisscrossed the sky, and a phalanx of trucks lurched across the fields behind them.

"There's no fight left in these Germans," Mykhailo said, walking a few metres to Maurice's left.

"Remember those boys yesterday?" said Oleh Vovk, next to Mykhailo. "They ran out of that bunker, waving their hands? They begged for mercy."

Maurice remembered. They could not have been more than 16 years old. But they were wearing the black uniform of the SS. The boys had fallen to their knees, weeping, their hands high over their heads. A commissar had come up. "Names and unit," he said. Before the boys could finish telling him, he drew his sidearm and shot each one in the head.

In 1941, the Germans executed every political officer they took prisoner, Maurice thought. *I guess it's no use expecting different behaviour from the commissars now.*

They walked across the rolling fields, spread out, watching the ground carefully. The weather was warm for April, the sun high and bright. Maurice turned to watch a young officer whistling as he walked along a country road, when he heard a crackling noise from ahead. The top of the officer's head blew away in a red shower. Maurice and the other soldiers threw themselves to the ground. Sergeants and corporals shouted "get down!" and "enemy ahead!"

Maurice heard more crackling as he threw himself into a shallow depression in the field. Something tugged at his pack as his chest hit the soil, winding him. He lifted his head and could see a gun barrel sticking out of a narrow slit in the ground.

The Reds returned fire uselessly. The slit was too small to allow anyone to hit it effectively at that range. But the Reds were angry, now. Obeying their training, they crept forward, fired a few shots and then rolled away to let another man fire from a different angle. The machine gun swept back and forth, killing three exposed Red soldiers. Then someone fired an anti-tank shell directly at the bunker.

The explosion blew earth and concrete high into the air. Maurice held onto his helmet and hoped no rocks would fall onto him. When he looked up again, Soviet men were running toward the destroyed enemy bunker.

He ran for it himself, rifle aimed ahead. There was no need. Bodies in black uniforms lay, broken, in the now-exposed strong point. Two were still alive, crawling pitifully for steps that led down to a tunnel. Oleh Vovk and another Red Army man shot them, repeatedly, until they stopped moving.

A commissar came up then and administered a single shot to the head of each SS man. Maurice turned away, his stomach churning.

"Close call, Maurice," said Mykhailo, patting him on the back.

"Yes," he agreed.

"No, for you, comrade. Look at your pack."

Maurice craned his head around, but could not see his backpack. He slid it off. What the hell is he talking about?

With the pack on the ground, he could see the answer: three neat holes through the top of the pack where bullets had passed through.

They reached a farming village in the afternoon. Maurice saw Commissar Sorkin say a few words to the captain, who then passed them to the lieutenants. Schwatchko passed the orders to Sergeant Nikolaev and the boys.

"Go into the houses and get some food. And whatever else we can use," he said. "Go two by two."

"Just take things?" Mykhailo asked.

"You can say 'please' if you want to," Schwatchko answered. He took Grigory Kornev with him. Corporal Shewchuk took Old Stepan.

"Mykhailo and I will check out that farmhouse over there," Maurice said to the corporal. He pointed at a trim, neat white house set a little apart from the village. He wasn't sure whether the corporal had heard him, but Shewchuk did not object when Maurice cuffed Mykhailo on the shoulder and started toward the house. "Don't wait for us," he joked. "We'll catch up."

The farmhouse was modest by German standards, but spectacular compared to most houses in Ukraine. It had escaped war damage so far, other than having the surrounding fields churned by treads, wheels and thousands of marching feet and the fences knocked down by tanks.

Maurice stepped onto the small porch and knocked boldly on the door.

A small, very nervous looking man in a white shirt and black vest opened. "Good morning, Herr bauer (farmer)," said Maurice in his polite, high-school German. "Would you have some bread for a hungry soldier of liberation?"

The farmer said nothing, but stood to one side. Maurice followed the farmer to his kitchen, where a thin blond woman stood beside the counter and two young girls hid behind her. Maurice nodded at Mykhailo, who quickly checked in every room, rifle aimed. "It's clear," he called in a minute. "No one else here."

Maurice sat down at the kitchen table, setting his rifle within reach. He marveled at how clean and neat the whole house was. It had been months since he had seen any building that wasn't an army edifice, rough and ready—they were clean, but not like this house. There were little decorations all over, crocheted doilies on the table and counters. There was running water and even an electric light on the ceiling—although it wasn't working now.

Mykhailo sat at the table across from Maurice. "Is this the whole family?" he asked.

Maurice repeated the question in German.

"Our older son was killed two years ago in Ukraine," the farmer said, putting his arm around his wife's shoulders.

"Ukraine!" Mykhailo exclaimed in poor, heavily accented German. "That's where we're from."

Maurice shook his head. "They don't want to hear that now, Myko," he said in Russian. He turned to the farmer and went back to German. "Do you have anything to eat?"

The farmer's wife put a plate of bacon on the table, another stacked with hand-sliced bread, and then returned to the wood stove to make tea. Famished, Maurice and Mykhailo tore into the unexpected feast.

The farmer ushered his wife and daughters out of the kitchen. Maurice moved his chair so that he could see where they sat, in the living room. *Where would they go? Outside are nothing but more Red Army soldiers.*

The farmer returned to the kitchen table. "A Russian who speaks such polite German. Where are you from?"

"Ternopyl," Maurice answered and sipped his tea. He wished there was some lemon to put in it.

"Where is that?"

"It's east of L'viv. What you Germans called Lemberg, in Galizia—which we call Halychyna."

The farmer nodded. "So you're not Russian yourself, then, are you? You're from the Ukraine."

"Just 'Ukraine.' Not 'the Ukraine.' Like 'Germany,' not 'the Germany.'"

"I see." The farmer took a bottle of clear liquor from a cabinet and poured them each a small glass. "Then, my Ukrainian liberators, let us drink to the end of the war."

The farmer's wife stood in the kitchen doorway when the farmer poured another round of the clear liquor. The farmer himself became friendlier with each successive toast. "To freedom! To the Soviet Union! To a free Germany!" When he said "To comrade Stalin!" Maurice felt a little pang, but Mykhailo had no trouble downing another shot.

Even the farmer's wife seemed to warm up to the Red Army soldiers after she drank a few toasts. She smiled at Mykhailo and raised a glass at the third toast "to the end of the war!"

When Maurice looked out the window again, the sun had begun to set. The shadow of the barn fell across the fields and he could no longer see, nor hear the rumble of the moving Red Army. He felt tipsy, and Mykhailo was trying to dance, without music, with the farmer's older daughter.

Maurice picked up his rifle, feeling foolish. *I can't believe I let that get out of my grasp.* "Come on, Myko, we need to find a place to spend the night," he said, his voice slow and thick.

"You can stay in the hayloft over the barn," said the farmer. "You may as well—you'll never catch up with the army tonight, in the dark."

"Sounds good to me, Maurice," Mykhailo said in Ukrainian.

"It could be dangerous," Maurice said.

"Bah," Mykhailo waved his hand dismissively, and nearly fell over. "If the farmer here hasn't tried anything yet, he won't. Besides, the whole area is full of ... of ... of us! Wha's he gonna do?"

"It's not the farmer I'm worried about," Maurice muttered, but the wife was standing with an armload of blankets. The farmer had opened the door and was gesturing them out.

Mykhailo was first out the door, and Maurice had to carry out his rifle for him. The farmer led them across the darkening field and into the neatest, cleanest barn Maurice had ever seen. Inside, he lit a small gas lantern and led them up a slanting ladder, carefully balancing the blankets.

Mykhailo followed him into the loft. Maurice let the farmer's wife carry a basket of food up to the loft, and then checked outside the barn before climbing after them.

He found Mykhailo was pushing straw together to make a bed. He spread a blanket over it. The farmer gave him a bottle of wine. Myko pulled out the cork and guzzled. The farmer's wife put the basket of food down on the loft floor and disappeared down the ladder-stairs.

"Stay, my friend," said the farmer, and Maurice could see he was tipsy, too. "You'll be safe." Then he followed his wife.

There was a square door about chest-high in the front of the loft, for loading hay. Maurice pushed it open and watched the farmer and his wife cross the yard to their house. They both turned on the doorstep and looked up at the barn. The farmer waved to him as his wife went into the house. Feeling foolish and uneasy, Maurice waved back as the farmer went into his house.

At least, the loft is warm and dry. It was early for going to bed, but he felt weary from months of marching and fighting. Lice crawled through his clothes and his hair and he knew he stank. *It would be a shame to lay my dirty body down in such a clean house as that.*

He looked in the basket: half a loaf of rye bread and another half-full bottle of wine. Mykhailo was busy downing his half-bottle. Maurice took one of the blankets and spread it over some straw near the door. He settled down to keep watch, although the east-facing door did not give him a broad field of vision.

"I'll take first watch," he said. Mykhailo muttered something and within minutes filled the loft with snoring.

It was a clear night. Maurice watched the stars come to life over the farm and wondered what time it was. The Red Army issued watches only to officers. *How long should I wait till I wake Mykhailo? Too soon and he'll still be drunk. But I have to wake him before I fall asleep.*

Loud banging startled him, and he sat up with a shock when he saw the sunlight streaming into the open loft door. The banging came again, accompanied by voices shouting—in Russian. He peeked out the door, careful to stay hidden, and saw four uniformed men at the door of the farmhouse. A truck with Red Army stars on it was parked in front of the house, two Red Army riflemen at the ready beside it.

One of the men at the house bashed on the door with the butt of his rifle again, and shock froze Maurice's body when he saw the red stripe around the officer's cap.

NKVD. The security police.

He heard the door splinter and then saw it swing inward. The three soldiers pushed their way in. The officer reached in and pulled the farmer out. "Who's inside?" he barked in

Russian, the repeated himself in crude, Russian-accented German.

"Just my wife and daughters," the farmer whined, his voice shaking. The Russian officer pushed him, and he fell off the steps. The NKVD officer drew his sidearm. "Honestly, Herr Commandant," the farmer whined from his hands and knees. "There is no one here but my family."

"Have you seen any Soviet soldiers lingering around here?"

Maurice could feel his heart pounding in his throat. *Please.*

"Nein, Herr Commandant," the farmer said. "No Russian soldiers stopped here until you came. Yesterday, troops marched past, tanks and trucks, too. But no one stopped here."

Maurice could hear the soldiers searching: crashing, breaking glass and crockery. When the soldiers came out, each carried something: food, a coat, a pair of high leather boots.

"Search the barn," the officer ordered. Maurice shook Mykhailo and covered his mouth. Then he buried them both in straw and held his breath as the soldiers tramped through the building. He listened as they pushed the cattle out below. He imagined some of the sounds were bayonets stabbing into piles of straw in the stalls.

After what felt like hours, he heard one say "There's no one here, comrade commissar. Just a few cows and some chickens, sir."

"Take the chickens," the commissar said. Maurice heard more tramping and crashing, followed by the roar of the truck. Still, he waited.

"Maurice?" The straw muffled Mykhailo's voice. "Think it's safe to come out?"

"Shut up," he whispered, and waited longer.

He heard the barn door open and close, then steps on the ladder. "Soldiers?" came the farmer's voice. Maurice pushed straw away from his face to see the farmer's head poking above the opening in the loft floor. "They're gone. It's safe, now. You had better go."

Maurice stood, straw falling off him. He kicked Mykhailo, gently, under the straw. He got up, too, looking bemused. "Please, go as fast as you can. I don't want this kind of trouble. In fact, avoiding it is exactly why I let you stay here."

"You let us stay here because you are afraid of us," Maurice said. He picked up his rifle from under the straw, slung it over his shoulder, picked up the basket with the bread and wine and climbed down out of the loft. He heard Mykhailo follow him.

On the ground floor of the barn, the farmer sadly surveyed the mess left by the soldiers. All the stalls were open and empty. Straw was strewn across the once neat floor, and the tools, once hung so precisely, lay everywhere. Several were broken on the floor. "I'm sorry," Maurice said.

The farmer shrugged. "They would have done this whether you were here or not," he said. "Now please, go."

The two Red Army soldiers made sure their uniforms were as straight as they could be. Maurice drained the last of the wine as they walked westward from the farm. He broke the remaining bread and gave half to Mykhailo, who pointed to another marching unit of Red Army men. They hustled to catch up and blended in. No one asked where they had come from. They just continued toward Berlin.

The Red Army never minds anyone joining, but they're murderously jealous when anyone tries to leave.

Berlin

April 1945

The Canadians, British, Americans and French had liberated France and driven the Germans against the Rhine, crossing the river in March 1945. The Canadians, with British and free Polish and The Canadians, British, Americans and French had liberated France and driven the Germans against the Rhine, crossing the river in March 1945. The Canadians, with British and free Polish and Czechoslovakian units, spent April fighting to liberate the Netherlands.

Königsberg fell in April and the Soviet armies in Germany pushed farther west. They paused on the eastern side of the Oder River for over a month, waiting for their supply lines to catch up. In a desperate attempt to hold the Soviets back, the Germans released the water from an upstream reservoir, turning the Oder's flood plain into a swamp.

To the south, other Soviet army fronts smashed through Hungary, Czechoslovakia and Yugoslavia. They conquered Vienna by mid-April and drove toward Bavaria.

To the west, the Americans encircled Field Marshal Model's Army Group B, taking 300,000 prisoners, and reached the Elbe River by mid-April. They decided not to push farther east, since according to the agreements among the Allies, Eastern Germany would be occupied by the Soviets. Instead, the French and American forces pushed into Bavaria, taking Munich and even reaching Czechoslovakia. The Americans and Soviets met at the banks of the Elbe by the end of April.

The Germans hung on in Amsterdam, in Breslau, and in the south, defying the Allied advances. They fought harder on the eastern front, preferring to surrender to what they knew had to be gentler mercies of the Western Allies.

They were right to dread Russian retribution.

Once Konigsberg fell, the Soviets concentrated three entire army "Fronts," or groups of armies, in an arc for the final assault on Berlin. The Soviets had 2,500,000 men, 6,000 tanks, 7,500 aircraft, 41,000 artillery pieces and more than 3,200 Katyusha multi-rocket launchers. The defenders of Berlin faced them with 100,000 men, including aged veterans in the *Volksturrm* and teenagers in the Hitler Youth, fewer than 600 tanks, 2,600 artillery pieces, under 700 anti-aircraft guns, and almost no remaining airplanes.

In the early morning of April 16, the Soviet Red Army launched a massive bombardment of the Seelow Heights, east of the city. Miles away, Maurice heard the shells exploding. He and the men in his unit could see the glow from searchlights meant to blind the defenders.

As the sun rose and burned off the mist, they saw black smoke hanging over the city. Though they didn't know it, to the west the Americans and British were bombing Berlin from the sky.

Despite the overwhelming superiority of men and machines, the Red Army got mired in the flooded ground below the Seelow Heights. The Germans responded with a barrage of their own that tore apart the front Soviet ranks. They advanced only six kilometres the first day, losing thousands of men.

The Germans held on for two days. On April 18, 1945, the Fourth Panzer Army fled when the First Belorussian Front broke through their final defences.

The First Ukrainian Front to the south made better progress, taking the city of Forst the first day. It drove west and encircled Berlin, and then turned to attack the capital itself.

On April 20, the captain of Maurice's new unit—whose name he had not learned, yet—passed on the order for the company to move west. Sometime in the dark predawn, the bombers roared across the Oder, and Maurice watched the flashes and fires in the distance. Once the bombers were gone, "Stalin's Organs," the Katyusha rocket launchers, sent volleys of death across the river.

As the sun rose behind them, the Red Army got the orders to move across the river. With rifles ready, Maurice's unit marched over the bridge behind a group of tanks. He tried not to think about charges under the bridge blowing when they were halfway across, spilling them into the freezing black water below.

But they made it across the river to find, beyond the Soviet positions at the edge of their bridgehead, the torn remnants of the German defences. They passed smoking trucks and tanks, twisted metal, craters of concrete and brick, the remains of bunkers. As the sun rose higher, Maurice saw that the ground appeared to undulate from the river and the roads, and realized the waves were all that was left of trenches and defences made by the Germans. The Soviet shells and rockets had torn up the ground, leaving a scarred, dead landscape. Broken tree stumps poked out of mounds of ash.

Maurice kept his eyes on the back of the man in front of him, away from the body parts in his peripheral vision and his imagination.

The shelling had wrecked the road, as well. Tanks and men had to pick their way around gigantic holes. Men fell down the crumbling sides of bomb craters, to be pulled up by their comrades. Tanks slid down and sent up billowing clouds of dust as they struggled to climb out. Worse were the horses that fell in, pulled by the wagons that toppled over the edge, breaking legs and necks. Corporals and sergeants put them out of their misery as men transferred the contents of their wagons.

Overhead, Soviet fighters buzzed, prowling for a decimated Luftwaffe.

The Germans answered the early morning bombardment with shells bursting behind the leading edge of the Soviet advance, landing with pinpoint accuracy, blasting apart trucks and shredding men.

"Take cover," the corporal called. The men threw themselves into a shell crater, aiming rifles and submachine guns over the lip. To the west they could see Panzers, Tigers and Stugs sheltering behind broken walls of buildings in the skeleton of a town. A muzzle flashed. A few seconds later and a hundred metres away, debris and dust erupted.

The men in Maurice's unit hunched low. Somewhere behind him, others readied mortars. A cannon barked, officers yelled commands, and within a minute the Soviet and German armies were engaged in a full artillery duel.

The Germans' position was hopeless. The Soviets outnumbered the defenders more than ten to one. Maurice watched multiple parallel fiery streaks of Katyushas silence the German artillery in a matter of minutes.

Heavy Soviet KV tanks rumbled past Maurice's position. A shell hit one, stopping it dead and tearing a hole in its front deck. The tank next to it fired its cannon and accelerated.

More tanks came, diving into the craters and up the other side. "Come on, boys," the sergeant shouted, and five men jumped onto the deck of a T-34.

Maurice and three other men scrambled onto another tank. Maurice clung to the handlebar on the side. His feet, on the plating over the treads, vibrated as the tank crushed obstacles on the ground.

A man Maurice only knew by his nickname, Hound, clung to the same bar, but his legs dangled over the side, swinging close to the tank treads. Maurice braced his feet as well as he could, tucked his rifle under his left arm and reached for Hound's arm. The tank jolted at that moment and Maurice's foot slid close to the edge of the plating. Hound's right hand let go of the bar. Maurice leaned farther, grabbing the other man's greatcoat. The tank lurched again and Maurice nearly fell off along with Hound. He tightened his grip on the handlebar and hauled the man up beside him.

Hound's brown eyes were wide with fear. He stared at Maurice for a long moment, then nodded as he re-established his grip on the handlebar. "Spasivo," he shouted over the roar of the engine. "Thank you."

A shell erupted twenty metres behind them, showering them with dust. Maurice nodded as the tank fired its cannon. The explosion shook the whole machine, threatening to knock them off again, and Maurice held onto Hound's coat with one hand and to the handlebar with the other.

A corporal on the other side of the deck fired his submachine gun forward, joined by the tank's forward machine gun. The tank accelerated into a cloud of smoke and dust. When it cleared, the men on the deck ducked behind the turret seconds before the tank smashed through a crumbling brick wall.

They were in what may have once been a factory. The corporal on the deck fired a short burst of his submachine gun, and then the rest of the men were shooting at grey-clad soldiers who had been hiding in the shell of the building. Maurice fired at a man in a dark grey uniform when he raised a rifle. The SS man lurched backward as four bullets from different directions hit him at once.

The tank braked hard, sending Maurice tumbling to the ground. He rolled as he hit the ground to absorb the impact and stopped where he was looking into a pair of blue eyes under a flared helmet. Only when he jumped back did he realize that the man who stopped his fall was dead. Maurice grabbed the Luger from the body's right hand and ran back to the tank.

It cleared the far side of whatever the brick building had been and roared down a street. Maurice wondered for a moment what the name of the town was, but then he heard more gunfire. He ran forward, joining a small group of soldiers looking for cover in the bomb-blasted town. Fires burned on piles of rubble that had once been houses and shops. A grenade detonated to his left and a Soviet soldier fell.

Maurice and three other men threw themselves behind a pile of bricks and broken masonry as a machine gun drew a path in the dust around them. "Snipers," said one man.

"Not with a submachine gun," said another, a corporal. He raised his head to take a look, just far enough for a single bullet to penetrate his eye. He fell onto his back.

Maurice tasted something bitter and burning in the back of his throat. One of the other men looked at him, nodded, and the three remaining rose up as one, firing at a second-storey window. They dropped again before the German could respond.

More machine gun fire hit the pile of bricks in front of them. When it paused, a young Soviet lieutenant threw himself against the bricks beside Maurice. *Where did he come from?*

"There are two of the bastards on the first floor," he said. He pointed at one of the Soviet soldiers, who carried a submachine gun. "You give us covering fire. You two," he indicated Maurice and the other living man beside him, "come with me into the building. We're going to kill those fucking Nazis."

This is not the riskiest order I've had in this war, Maurice thought. *But it's close.*

The officer took his sidearm revolver from its holster, unstrapped his helmet and raised it with his left hand over the top of the rubble. The German machine gun fired again, two short bursts that missed. "Now," the lieutenant said.

The man with the submachine gun leaned to the side of the rubble and fired at the window where the enemy fire had come from. At the same moment, the lieutenant leaped around the other side of the pile, Maurice and the other man behind him. They dashed across the street, praying not to be hit, and reached the bullet-scarred building.

It had been a small tenement, its front door long since destroyed. The lieutenant led them to a wide staircase that rose eight steps before doubling back for another eight.

He paused on the second-storey landing, crouching low beside a banister that afforded not even the illusion of cover. Maurice and the other man crouched just behind him, looking along a hallway with doors on both sides. *Which one is the right one?* Maurice wondered.

The lieutenant seems to know. He pointed to the second door on the right, then nodded at Maurice and the other man. They pulled back the bolts on their rifles. The lieutenant stepped silently to the door, holding his revolver in front of him. He stood to one side of it, aimed his sidearm at the doorknob, and signaled to the men behind him.

They all fired at the same time, tearing three holes through the wooden door. Maurice and the other man pulled the bolts back on their rifles as quickly as they could as the lieutenant kicked the door open.

But he miscalculated. As the door sprang open, a single shot rang out and the lieutenant crumpled to the floor. Maurice and the other soldier fired their rifles through the door at the same time and saw a lone man in an SS uniform fall to the floor, dropping a submachine gun. Beside him another black uniformed body lay bleeding from a hole in its head.

Maurice turned to the lieutenant on the floor. The bullet had hit him in the stomach. Blood soaked the front of his uniform and spread in a growing puddle on the floor of the hallway. He looked at Maurice with fading eyes. "Did we get the bastards?" he asked. Blood leaked from the corners of his mouth.

"You got one, and we got the other," Maurice said. He helped the lieutenant lie down.

The young officer coughed, and more blood flowed down his chin. He took one last breath that bubbled in his throat, and then he did not move again.

"Take his knees, I'll take his shoulders," Maurice said to the other man, who had slung the German submachine gun over one shoulder and was busy taking the boots from one of the SS men to replace his own.

They picked up the lieutenant and headed for the stairs when an explosion rocked the building. The man at the lieutenant's knees dropped him and ran. "Wait!" Maurice called after him, answered only by more explosions, farther away.

"They've started shelling again. Get out of here!" called the third man from the entrance of the tenement.

Maurice lifted the lieutenant's shoulders and dragged his legs down the stairs. His feet flopped comically and sickeningly over each step. When he reached the landing, the third man, the one who had provided covering fire with his submachine gun, urged him out again. "Forget him, unless you want a shell to land on your head."

"Who's shelling?"

"We are, you idiot! Forget him. He's dead. It won't matter to him anymore."

Maurice grabbed the lieutenant's Nagant revolver and shoved it into a pocket. It was only then that he remembered the Luger he had taken from the German he had fallen onto. It seemed so long ago.

"Come on," the third Red soldier urged before he sprinted out the door, heading down the shattered street toward the Soviet lines. Maurice ran after him as explosions rocked the ground.

The town had put up expected resistance, so the Red Army field commanders issued orders to pull their men out. They then fired the heavy gun before all the Soviet soldiers had time to get out.

Hundreds of cannon and mortars and Katyushas opened up, reducing the town to a pile of broken masonry, even its medieval centre. The Red Army pushed past the smoking remains, closer to Berlin.

By April 22, the Soviet artillery was in range to strike the capital. A Soviet war correspondent reported that the bombardment began at exactly 8:30 a.m. Ninety-six shells fell in the centre of Berlin in a few minutes. The Soviet armies encircled the city by April 25. The next day, two armies attacked the airport. The Germans fought back, hard, slowing the advance, but it was hopeless. They had lost more than half the 100,000 soldiers they had defending the city when the battle began.

The Germans and Soviets fought house to house and hand to hand. On April 20, the Red Army attacked the Reichstag—ironically, because it had not been used since the Nazis had burned it in 1933. Still, the SS had fortified it and fought room to room. They also set up heavy guns on the roof of a tower in the nearby Berlin Zoo to fire on the attackers.

In and around Berlin, fanatics and SS men who knew they would not survive capture by the Reds continued to fight, either to kill as many of the communists they hated as possible, or to try to be captured by the Western Allies.

Hitler married his mistress, Eva Braun, on April 29. The next day, they both committed suicide in the Fuhrerbunker. The Fuhrer's last will and testament named Admiral Karl Donitz President of the Reich, and Joseph Goebbels Chancellor.

The German armies fought on. By May 1, they had fewer than 10,000 men left, concentrated around the Tiergarten, a large park in the centre of the city.

North of the city, the army of which Maurice was part kept the remnants of the Panzer Armies at bay. Maurice's company oversaw thousands of German prisoners marching into improvised camps, fields surrounded by barbed wire and well-armed Russians looking for revenge.

On May 1, Chancellor Goebbels dictated a letter to Red Army General Vasily Chuikov, Commander of the 8th Guards Army and the Soviet forces in Berlin, reporting Hitler's death and asking for a cease-fire. General Hans Krebs delivered it under a white flag. Chuikov rejected the request, insisting on unconditional surrender.

Meanwhile, the Red Army, the U.S. Army Air Force and the Royal Air Force continued to pound Berlin. Fighting continued north and south of the city, in northern Italy, Yugoslavia, Austria, Bavaria and Holland. American and Soviet armies met at the Elbe River at points north and south of Berlin.

On the night of May 1, the remaining German troops in Berlin tried to break out, hoping to escape the Reds and surrender to the Americans, Canadians and British. Most did not make it.

By May 2, the Red Army killed the last of the Reichstag defenders and controlled the building. The next morning, two soldiers re-enacted the raising of the hammer-and-sickle over the Reichstag for photographers.

General Helmut Weidling, commander of the Berlin defences, surrendered unconditionally to General Chuikov on May 2. On the same day, the German forces north of Berlin, and forces in northwestern Germany and Denmark surrendered to the Western Allies. German forces in Italy and Austria surrendered to the Americans on May 3.

It took until May 5 for the Germans in the Netherlands to surrender to Canadian General Charles Foulkes, the same day that Hitler's second-in-command, Hermann Goering, surrendered at the Austrian border. The next day, the fortress city of Breslau (now Wroclaw, Poland) surrendered to the Soviets.

Thirty minutes later, General Alfred Jodl, on Reichchancellor Donitz's instructions, offered to surrender all forces fighting the Western Allies—in effect, a separate peace, allowing the Germans to continue resisting the Soviet Union. The Supreme Allied Commander, General Dwight Eisenhower, responded that unless the Germans surrendered unconditionally, he would order western lines closed to the Germans, forcing them to surrender to the Soviet Union.

No German soldier wanted to surrender to the communists. In the early morning of May 7, 1945, Jodl signed the unconditional surrender for all German forces to the Allies. In Berlin, Field Marshal Wilhelm Keitel signed a surrender document for General Georgi Zhukov.

But it wasn't quite over. The last man Hitler named as Commander in Chief of the Army, Ferdinand Schorner, continued fighting in Czechoslovakia. He deserted his post on May 8 as Europe began celebrating V-E Day. The Soviets launched the overwhelming Prague Offensive, and the last German units, Army Group Centre, surrendered on May 11.

There were other pockets of fighting by Nazi fanatics, but the war was over.

It had left more than twenty million dead men, women and children.

In a camp east of Berlin, Maurice's unit had orders to guard refugees—Germans, mostly, whose homes had been destroyed by the fighting, or commandeered by Red Army officers and commissars.

Days before the fighting ended, Maurice and his comrades received orders very different from what they had heard for the past several months. "We're going to clear the roads," a new commissar said. He was short and prematurely balding, and he walked with a painful-looking limp.

Within hours, the unit was working alongside local people, clearing rubble and smashed vehicles from major roads. Commissary units fed the locals alongside the soldiers, and Maurice saw other teams repairing buildings to provide some housing for the refugees. He saw a line of civilians, mostly women, stretching for a block outside a new soup kitchen, where soldiers doled out whatever food they could provide.

But at night, groups of Red Army soldiers prowled the streets. They broke into houses that still stood intact, and raped women as old as eighty, as young as eight.

"Come with us, Maurice," said Pavel, another private in Maurice's new unit. He was very young, thin and usually very angry. "The fighting's over. Let's have some fun."

But this was not what Maurice considered fun. "No, thanks, Pavel," he answered.

"What are you, a faggot?" Pavel leered.

Maurice shook his head, fighting to stay calm. "Got a girl back home in Minsk," he lied. So far, the Russian boys in this unit had not questioned him when he said he was from Belorussia, not Ukraine.

"So?" Pavel shrugged. "She won't know if you don't tell her."

Pavel and four other Russian soldiers returned a few hours later, reeking of liquor, piss and sex, their pockets bulging. "Look at this stuff," Pavel said, dumping jewelry and silverware on the ground. "I told you that you should come with us. Fucking Germans are so rich. Why did they have to invade Russia? Fucking greedy, that's what they are."

"You took this from the locals? You could be shot for that. There are orders."

Pavel barked a laugh. "Are you joking? The fucking commissar was there. He took the most of all." He held up a gold ring with a purple stone. "Nice, isn't it? This ugly hausfrau gave it to me so I wouldn't touch her."

The ring looked relatively cheap to Maurice, but to someone from a collective farm, like Pavel, it was a treasure. "So, you left her alone?" he asked, dreading the answer.

"Fuck, yes. She was fat! I fucked her daughter instead. She was sweet. She loved it." He rolled his eyes and cooed, wrapping his arms around Maurice in horrible mimicry. "Ooh, ooh," he whined. "You should have heard her."

"You speak German?" Maurice asked.

"Fuck, no," Pavel waved his hand dismissively. "Not a word. But I know when a woman loves fucking."

Maurice thought more about how to get away from the Red Army.

Rejection

May 1945

No gardens bloomed. No window boxes proved the homeowner's gardening skill in May. The sunshine was warm, but there wasn't a living tree on the Unter den Linden, the street named for the trees that once lined its length.

Maurice picked his way through the shattered city, climbing over pieces of buildings and statues, dodging the trucks and jeeps that zipped officiously along the few streets where tanks and construction machines had cleared paths through the rubble. Water dribbled from broken hydrants and from the ends of pipes where bombs had blasted the streets into craters. Few windows contained any glass. No streetlights worked, but aside from official jeeps, Land Rovers and trucks, and the occasional tank, there was no traffic.

Gradually, he made his way to the Charlottenburg section of the former Nazi capital, the British-occupied zone. He found the British headquarters, in a once-white, five-storey office building with a concave-curving front.

Official and army vehicles made a barrier across the front. British soldiers stood guard beside the broad main doors, through which streamed men in uniform in both directions.

Long lines of people in civilian clothes stood along walls in various places on the main floor. Non-commissioned British soldiers bustled along the corridors, bearing messages. Occasionally, he saw French or American officers. He stood up straighter when he saw a brown uniform with maple leaves on the sleeves, but the tall man disappeared around a corner before Maurice could catch his eye.

Two Soviet officers strode down the hall. Maurice tried to fade into the wall until they passed him.

He stopped a friendly-looking sergeant, who directed him to an office on the second floor. He got in a lineup and finally stood in front of a young, blond lieutenant behind a small wooden desk. He summoned his best English to explain his case.

"I'm sorry, Private," said the lieutenant. "Majah Owens cannot see you without an appointment. Can you come tomorrow at—" he looked down at an appointment book placed precisely in the centre of the desk—"ten o'clock?"

Maurice thanked the lieutenant and strode out of the building as quickly as he could without drawing attention to himself. Frustration burned behind his ears. *I should be used to waiting by now. One thing that unites all armies in every country in the world is the way they make you wait.*

He made his way back to the centre of Berlin, occupied by the Soviet Red Army. The city looked unreal, a living nightmare of blasted buildings, cratered streets and military vehicles. Hundreds of thousands of soldiers from around the world jammed the streets. Maurice dodged as an American jeep roared down the centre of a cleared street, swerving drunkenly from one side to the other, narrowly missing twisted lampposts. He saw grinning GIs and two desperate-looking young women, their blouses blowing open. The men held bottles of wine.

He passed groups of soldiers drinking beer. Along one less-damaged street, more GIs smoked at open-air cafés and bars, chatting up pretty young girls with haunted eyes.

Two weeks had passed since Hitler had committed suicide and the Germans had surrendered unconditionally to the Allies, after the Red Army had conquered half the city and killed most of its defenders.

Fighting continued after the formal surrender. Fanatics continued to fight from isolated bunkers or defended positions. Stubborn German occupiers continued to fight the Canadians in the Netherlands until May 5, and even a day later opened fire on celebrations in Amsterdam. In Czechoslovakia, resistance fighters rose up against the German occupiers as the Red Army began the Prague Offensive. Colonel-General Carl Hilpert only surrendered to the Soviets in the Courland Pocket, near Memel, Lithuania on V-E Day, May 8.

The war was over, and the occupation began. The Red Army set about burying the 18,000 men it had lost in the Battle for Berlin.

Walking back to his unit in eastern Berlin, Maurice remembered how his commanders had given their men almost completely free rein in Berlin. The commissar—Maurice still hadn't learned his name—had said, "We were strict about respect for civilians in Lithuania and Poland. But now, we have defeated the German pigs." He held up a poster depicting a proud Red soldier. The caption read "The hour of our revenge has struck!"

"Take what you need from the Berliners. Take what you want."

Two hours after leaving Charlottenburg, he arrived back at his unit's camp in the eastern suburbs of the city. A disorderly array of small tents gathered around the mobile mess kitchen—really a large horse-drawn wagon—all set up in a field that bore more than one bomb crater. He had missed lunch, so he went to the kitchen, and one of the cooks gave him a bowl of soup and some bread. He made himself a cup of tea. No one asked him where he had been most of the day. The captain and the other officers had been drunk on German wine and beer for days.

"Hey, Maurice, give us a hand!" It was Danny, a friendly lout who was always in trouble with the sergeants because he always joked too loudly and was never any good at aiming a rifle. But he knew how to keep his head down, attached to his shoulders.

Danny and his friends had commandeered a horse and cart from some poor farmer. Two of the soldiers sat in the back, laughing. Maurice noticed they also had their rifles.

"What's going on, Danny?"

"I need you to speak to a German for us," Danny answered, slapping Maurice on the back as he climbed into the wagon. The cart jerked and rolled out of the camp. "This is Peter, and the one with the reins, there, is George."

"Where'd you get the wagon?"

"Liberated it from a farmer down the road. He's rich— or he was. You should see his house. Separate houses for the animals, indoor plumbing, the works. God, these Germans knew how to live, eh?" He passed Maurice a bottle of liberated German liquor.

Maurice didn't ask whether the German farmer still knew how to live.

The cart eventually rolled to another farm. Peter hopped down to open the gate and George steered toward the stables. The farmer and his wife, two hungry-looking blonds, came out of the barn, sullen and fearful. "Ask them where they keep their stores," said Danny.

From the look of them, Maurice doubted they had anything left, but asked anyway in his best German. "Where is your stored food?"

The farmer didn't reply. He gave Maurice a look full of sullen hate. Then he looked at Peter and Danny and the rifles in their hands. He jerked his head toward a silo attached to the barn.

George and Peter opened a low door in the side of the silo. "Hey, Danny, get a load of this!" Peter called.

Danny looked in the silo. "Tell him to get some sacks," he said. Maurice translated for the farmer. He stared at Maurice for a few seconds, then went into the barn. George picked up his rifle nervously, but the farmer returned, carrying empty burlap sacks. George and Peter took the bags and started filling them with grain from the silo—probably the last of the farmer's food.

"Help them!" Danny ordered the farmer, and even though he did not understand their language, he complied. "Come with me, Maurice," Danny said and went to the stable. Six milking cows stood, chewing their cuds. Danny beckoned Maurice, and they led the two biggest cows out and tied them to the back of the wagon.

"Not *two* cows!" said the farmer's wife.

"Shut up, Gerta," said the farmer without taking his eyes off Maurice. He watched silently as the four soldiers loaded eight sacks of grain and a few bales of hay onto the wagon. They climbed on and slowly trotted back down the path to the road without saying another word to the farmer. They passed the wine bottle until it was empty and Danny pitched it beside the road.

After a couple of jostling miles, they turned onto a narrow track through a thin screen of trees. Maurice heard the noise of hundreds of thousands of people, and smelled cooking and latrines and general uncleanliness—a smell Maurice had come to know over months and thousands of miles of marching with an army.

There was a high wire fence with two Red Army soldiers at the gates. The soldiers nodded the wagon through into a huge camp of tents and low shacks made of discarded metal and wood. And people—thousands of dirty, weary people staring at them.

It was a "displaced persons" camp, filled with people who had fled destroyed homes, along with Nazi slaves freed from factories, farms, and the homes of senior officers and bureaucrats.

Peter drove the wagon to one side of the camp where a small, dark-haired man greeted them. Danny jumped off the wagon and embraced him. "Hey, comrade, here you go!"

He explained to Maurice: "These fine people are from Lithuania, and they want to go home." Peter and George climbed down from the wagon as Danny introduced them to a gathering crowd. "These are the Lynisses," he said, indicating Mr. Lyniss, the small man, and his wife, a tiny, thin woman with a sharp nose and a weak chin. There were two dirty children and a bent old woman who pulled her shawl tight around her and shivered. Two cows, a load of hay, eight bags of grain and a wagon made them wealthy in the D.P. camp.

The Lynisses lost no time in loading their few belongings onto the wagon and driving it out of the camp. The guards said nothing.

Danny explained as the four soldiers walked back to their camp. "I met the old lady shivering on the side of the road yesterday, and helped her to get back here to this shitty D.P. camp. She told me they were from—oh, I don't remember, somewhere near Vilnius. They ran from their farm when the front came through there. The Nazis put them to work and they've been here in Berlin for months."

It was getting close to dinnertime and they were still far from their own camp. They were in the middle of a small suburb, a few houses with all the windows blown out. At a crossroads was a little collection of shops, including a café. They sat down and Danny banged on the table until the owner, a short, portly and bald older man, came out.

"Four cups of tea and a bottle of wine, and make it fast!" Danny demanded in rough German. The owner went back in without saying a word and returned with four cups, four glasses and a bottle of white wine. Danny snatched the wine and poured. "To victory!" he shouted and drained the glass in one gulp. The others did the same, and Danny refilled the glasses. The proprietor nearly ran back into the café.

Danny raised his glass again. "To the return of all refugees to their homes!" Again, they all downed their wine, and Danny refilled again, but the bottle was empty by the time he got to his own glass. "Hey, grandfather! Another bottle, and fast! *Bistro!*" The owner hurried out with another bottle. He had trouble pulling the cork because his hands were shaking.

"Bring us some food, too, man, and make it fast. We're hungry!"

"I have only cabbage soup and some bread," the owner protested.

Danny picked up his rifle. "Pretend we're officers."

The owner nodded and ran to the kitchen, yelling at the cook. Soon he returned with three loaves, some margarine and another bottle of wine. The men munched on the bread while sipping their tea. Maurice was disappointed—the tea was not hot enough. Out of pity for the proprietor, though, he did not say anything.

A few minutes later, the owner brought four bowls of soup, slopping some onto the table in his nervous haste. When the soldiers had finished that, the owner brought a platter of fried chicken and potatoes.

Maurice remembered the long days without food, the long marches with army rations. He remembered the dismay all the boys felt when a German shell hit a field kitchen. He realized then that Danny had no intention of paying for the food. *It's just as well. We have no money, anyway.*

Danny yelled for a fourth bottle of wine, and when they had drunk that, they all stood up unsteadily, picked up their rifles and left. The owner watched them, silently.

The next morning, Maurice woke lying on the ground, covered by the chenille tent; Danny and Peter were lying beside him. *How did I get here?*

He remembered, vaguely, staggering back to camp. Peter had another friend who had set up a still in the middle of a stand of trees on the edge of the camp, and who happily doled out *samohanke,* Ukrainian home-brewed whiskey.

Maurice stood up and went for a drink of water. Fog gradually burned off his memory of the night before. He remembered a major showing up at the still, and how all the boys had panicked until the major held out a mug for a shot. He had downed it, asked for another and they all relaxed.

Did the major join us in singing Ukrainian songs, too? Maurice could not be sure.

The sun was just coming up; Maurice washed his hands and face outside the latrine. The camp was beginning to stir. The sentries by the gate looked sleepy; their replacements would be coming soon. He made up his mind. He took his rifle to the gate and slapped one sentry on the shoulder. "I'm on duty today," in his best rural Russian accent.

The sentries look doubtful. "Just you?"

"Nikolai will be joining me soon. He's just in the latrine right now. You two can go on."

"We're supposed to stay until the next watch gets here."

"I'm here, *tovarisch*. Is this the first time you've stood watch all night?"

The sentry that Maurice had slapped on the shoulder nodded. "Got into a little trouble with the commissar. You know, that bastard Linsky."

"Go on, get some rest. It's okay, the war is over. No one's going to try to get in."

The sentries started to leave. "Okay ... who are you, anyway?" the second one asked.

"George Fedorov," Maurice answered. The sentries waved thank-you, then headed for the kitchen.

Maurice waited just until they were twenty yards away, looked around quickly, put down his rifle and walked as quietly as he could toward the road. He looked over his shoulder to make sure no one had noticed that the gate was unguarded. Then, as soon as he could, he ducked behind trees and moved away, walking fast, but not so fast that he would attract attention.

The sun rose; he could tell it would be a warm day. He took off his coat, rolled it and slung it over his shoulder. That, his uniform and his boots were all he had—those, plus the greatest treasure he owned: his Canadian birth certificate.

It took over an hour to reach Berlin. There were soldiers everywhere, but none were alone. But there was something else as prevalent as soldiers, though: debris. Maurice picked up a cloth pouch he found on the side of the road. He hoped that if anyone noticed him, he would look like a courier delivering a message.

It had been two weeks since Germany surrendered. The Allies were starting to restore some normalcy to Berlin. As he walked through the shattered streets, Maurice noticed that most of the broken water mains had been shut off and the streets were dry. Work crews consisting of German prisoners supervised by Soviet soldiers, picked up rubble and swept the streets. Others boarded up empty windows. A large crew swarmed over what Maurice thought must have been an old hotel. *Making it livable for high-ranking officers, probably.*

Back at the British headquarters in Charlottenburg, Maurice found the pleasant blond lieutenant at the tidy desk and sat down on a polished wooden bench. He was more than an hour early for his appointment. The lieutenant smiled and nodded at him, then busied himself with his papers again.

Maurice was used to waiting. He was a soldier, after all.

At precisely 10:00, the lieutenant ushered Maurice into a crowded office. Behind an ornate wooden desk sat Major Retent, a tall, thin man with a dark, thin moustache and an impossibly well-pressed uniform. On either side of him sat his aides: a portly, bald captain on the left and a nervous young lieutenant on the right. On one side of the room was a corporal behind a stenographic machine; on the other side, two non-commissioned officers sweated in the close quarters as they tried to keep a growing stack of files straight.

"Name, rank and unit," said the lieutenant.

"Maurice Bury," he answered, in English. "Private." *I should have said "lieutenant,"* he thought. "Soviet Red Army."

"What are you doing here, Private?" asked the Major. He had a very nasal voice.

"I need papers to go to Canada."

The major did not even look at him. He was studying some papers on the desk. "And why should you want to go to Canada instead of Russia?"

"Because I want to go home. I am not Russian, I am Canadian." That made the Major look up. Maurice was very conscious of his very non-Canadian-sounding accent.

"Canadian? What do you mean, 'Canadian'? You are wearing the uniform of the Soviet army."

Maurice was ready for that. "My birth certificate," he said, and put it on the desk in front of the Major. The Major appeared to study the big letters across the top that spelled "Dominion of Canada," then gave it to the captain, who passed it back to the lieutenant. The lieutenant gave it back to Maurice.

"Very interesting, Private Bury," said the Major, leaning forward with his hand under his chin. "Tell me, how does a Canadian end up in the Soviet Red Army?"

Maurice knew he couldn't tell his whole story, but he had rehearsed what he would say as he walked in from the camp. "I was born in Montreal in 1919. My parents had immigrated from western Ukraine, near Ternopyl, which was then under Poland. When I was nine, the depression came." The Major nodded at that and the captain wrote something down. "So my mother took my sister and me back to Ternopyl, where she still owned some land and we thought we would be better off.

"When the war came, Germany took that part of Poland. Then, when the Soviets returned in 1944, they took me into the army." There is so much more to the story, he thought. But more will get me killed.

"And now, you are here," said the Major.

"Yes."

"Jolly good bit of fighting you Russkies did, there."

"I'm not Russian," Maurice repeated. "I'm Canadian."

"Ah, yes, a Canadian. Of Russian descent, though."

"No, not Russian. Ukrainian."

"Quite. Little Russia, the Ukraine." Maurice inwardly winced at the Major's unintentional slight—or was it intentional? It did not matter. What was important was ...

"And now I would like to return home, to see my father."

The Major tapped his fingers together. "Your father is still in Canada?" Maurice nodded. "What about your mother? Don't you want to return to her, especially now that the war is over?"

"Things were peaceful in our village when I left. I know she's well. I received a letter from her recently." That was a lie. The Soviet Union, chaotic at the best of times, had had no reliable mail service since the war began.

"I see," the Major nodded. He straightened his back and said "I'm sorry, Private, but the British Commission simply cannot be transporting Soviet soldiers to wherever they wish to go. You can understand that it is simply against regulations." He reached for some more papers that the lieutenant held out. "If you do wish to return to Canada, you must first return to Russia with your unit, and then apply to emigrate from there. If you wish to fill out this form, we can begin processing your immigration request from here, to expedite it on our side, later."

Maurice was stunned. "But I am a Canadian citizen, not Russian. I am not a Soviet. I only want to return home."

"I understand, Private Bury," the Major said very patiently. "But I cannot help an allied soldier to desert his unit. If you follow the proper channels, in good time your request will, I am certain, be honoured. Perhaps if you would care to return in the afternoon, when Lieutenant Charles has some free time, the two of you can begin the request for immigration." He looked at another paper on his desk.

Maurice shook his head. Returning to Ukraine was impossible. But it would be useless to explain that to these officers. He pretended to agree to return yet again, and left the office.

He could not get out of the building fast enough. He felt as if a huge claw was squeezing his chest. He kept looking over his shoulder, dreading the sight of another Red Army uniform. Only once he got to the ruined street, among the wounded and traumatized people who staggered by, dodging army trucks and jeeps and tripping over debris, did he feel like he could breathe.

If Major Retent had known his whole story, would he have granted Maurice's request? Or would he have turned him over to the Red Army to be shot immediately?

"Stupid officers!" he shouted, but no one looked at him. There were too many broken people in that broken city for anyone to worry about one more man talking to himself.

Half-blind with increasing anger, Maurice stumbled through the rubble. I knew it would not be easy to get to Canada, but I didn't think the British would be part of the problem.

He found he had joined a general flow of people down the once-broad avenue, and he let the crowd carry him generally southward. Good: south is the American zone of occupation.

By afternoon, he reached a railway yard. He was surprised to see how undamaged it seemed. It was idle. Freight wagons sat on the tracks, open and empty. The crowd moved faster, and as he followed, Maurice realized they were converging on a series of open boxcars. With the rest of the crowd, Maurice started running.

The boxcars were filled with clothes, unused and unembellished *wehrmacht* uniforms once destined for the front lines, as well as boxes and crates of plain civilian pants, shirts and jackets, even socks and underwear. The Germans had always been particular about having good uniforms. The crowd rifled through torn-open boxes, taking what they could, stuffing clothing into bags or boxes or just throwing them over their shoulders. It was chaos.

Maurice knew what he had to do. Dropping his heavy Russian chenille to the ground—where it was immediately grabbed by another man—he replaced it with a long, grey German coat. He took a new shirt, new socks, new underwear and new pants, moving down the length of the boxcar, pushing through the crowd to grab what he needed. He went to a corner and, not caring who saw him, changed quickly. He was no longer a Soviet soldier, but just another refugee crowding the roads of Germany.

In the May sunshine, Maurice Bury, former Red Army soldier, former Ukrainian resistance fighter, former Soviet Red Army officer, and hoping to be a Canadian citizen again, followed the flow of the crowds south. He set his goal as Munich, where the American army occupied Bavaria.

Ingolstadt

June 1945

May turned into June as Maurice walked southwest toward Munich. The sun got hot, but Maurice held onto the German overcoat – the nights were cold and besides, it might just represent a turn in his luck.

The countryside continued its checkerboard pattern of picture-perfect farmland and rural villages next to devastated countryside, burned without a living thing left standing, featureless except for charred hulks of cars, trucks and tanks, and twisted piles of metal that were once airplanes.

Maurice felt more endangered than ever. The roads were jammed with people, desperate, hungry, lost and morose most of the time. Savage fights broke out among the refugees several times a day. Trucks and jeeps roared up and down the shattered highways, forcing the walking refugees to dodge out of the way. The vehicles represented all the victorious armies – British, American, French, even occasionally Canadians, but Maurice stayed out of their way as much as he could. More than once, he saw a Mercedes staff car or general's limousine with Wehrmacht markings still, filled with joy-riding, grinning GIs or Tommies.

Whenever a Red Army vehicle rumbled past, he hid in bushes or behind fences.

At night, Maurice sometimes joined a small camp of fellow refugees, as long as they didn't ask too many questions. On those nights, he could count on sharing a little food. Other than his time in the POW camp, he had never felt so hungry. In later years, he wouldn't be able to remember much of this time and couldn't recall at all how he found enough food to survive. But somehow, he did.

Gradually, the land changed from the rolling plains of northern Germany and Prussia to hillier, forested lands, then rose higher. He slowed until the roads suddenly began trending downhill. He didn't know it, but Maurice had entered the Danube valley.

Along the banks of the Danube was the town of Ingolstadt. Maurice found himself in the middle of a crowd of refugees that were being herded by the American Army toward a large fenced area outside the town.

Ingolstadt, eighty kilometres north of Munich, was one of the first Displaced Persons camps set up by the occupying Allies across Europe. The refugees flowed into the camp, finding places within the fences to set up a camp or to share a tent or other makeshift shelters. American soldiers directed men, refugees or escapees, in erecting small wooden buildings.

Although he was once again in a mass camp, Maurice was not afraid this time. He knew the Americans would feed them and eventually free them all. And even if they wanted to hold all the Germans, he was a Canadian citizen.

Before they could get food, the refugees had to endure a dusting by the American medical corps. "Preventing typhus," they said. "Take it or you don't get in and don't get fed." The refugees protested and made faces as the Americans spread the disinfectant dust on their faces, necks and hands.

Then they had to declare themselves before a small tribunal of a junior officer and non-commissioned clerks.

"Nationality?" asked the lieutenant, a thin young blond man with a thick accent that Maurice would later learn was southern. He would also learn that the real purpose of declaring nationality was to find Nazis, to prosecute them for the war.

"Canadian," said Maurice, assuming that would help him get back to Canada. But the lieutenant looked at him, puzzled.

"Canadian?" he repeated. "Did you say, 'Canadian'?"

"Yes, sir. Maurice Bury, Canadian citizen." He pointed at the "Canada" tag sewn onto his cap.

The lieutenant looked at his clerks, who looked as mystified as he did. He turned back to Maurice. "You're not German?"

"No."

"You're wearing a coat made for the German army."

"Yes, I know. I found it." Maurice realized this interview was not going well. He pulled out his Dominion of Canada birth certificate again and showed it to the officer.

The American just shook his head. "Sorry, that means you're not entitled to food from this camp."

Maurice was stunned. He couldn't even think of anything to say.

"This camp is for German and other national refugees, not for personnel of Allied countries," he explained. "It's the beginning of a reconstruction project to rebuild Germany." He leaned closer, an angry look beginning to form on his face. "Now, see here, I don't know why any Allied soldier would do such a thing in Germany these days, but if – " he leaned closer " – I say, if you are absent without leave from the Canadian army, I suggest you hightail it back to your unit!"

Maurice backed away, terrified. That was just too close to the truth. "No, no, I've never been in the army," he said, suddenly aware that his voice was too loud. "I am a Canadian, I was born in Montreal, and now I just want to— to get back home."

The blond lieutenant looked at him through narrowed eyes. "Look, you can stay tonight, get a meal. But tomorrow, you go find your unit in the Canadian army, wherever it is." He dismissed Maurice with a "Next!"

"Thank you." Maurice turned and walked to another lineup, this one leading to a huge open-air kitchen where more Americans were giving out soup and bread. His heart was pounding. The American lieutenant had accused him of deserting—which was technically true, at least the way the Soviet Red Army was bound to see it. *I never deserted my comrades during the fighting, no matter how tough the Germans were,* he told himself.

The camp was minimal. Over a parish hall, the Americans had hoisted their national flag, alongside another, red one. Maurice had to look at it for more than a minute before he recognized the image: the face of a gigantic black cat, eating a tank. He did not know it, but he had come upon the vaunted 692nd Tank Destroyer Battalion, the unit whose accurate artillery fire had allowed American infantry to cross the Rhine, and was the only unit to breach the Siegfried Line twice.

The senior officers had commandeered a large house near the parish hall as their headquarters, the junior officers were in nearby houses, and the enlisted men slept in the hall itself, or in tents erected on the church lawn. They gave the refugees tents in a large park they had fenced off. Others found corners in abandoned sheds and barns to sleep in.

Maurice wandered around the camp, looking for a dry, warm spot to sleep and listening to the conversations of small groups of people. They were all glum and wary. They would look at him only until he looked back, then turn away, unwilling to make contact. For them, the war was not over.

He found a shed that held gardening tools, presumably to maintain the park that was now a refugee camp. He and another young man stacked the shovels and rakes against the wall outside. Maurice spread his coat on the floor. The other man sat in a corner, leaning against the wall, and closed his eyes.

It's not as bad as the prison camp in Kharkiv, Maurice thought, lying on his side with his head on his arm as a pillow.

He and the other man had not exchanged a word.

Breakfast the next day was porridge. When he first looked at the unappetizing mess in his bowl, Maurice hoped it would be something like his mother's kasha, or buckwheat porridge. One taste dashed that hope. But at least there was tea, albeit without lemon.

After breakfast, Maurice wandered around the camp, simultaneously bored and worried that the lieutenant who had warned him that he could not stay long would see him and throw him out. He knew, though, that he would eventually have to find Canadian authorities if he hoped to get home, and avoid being taken by the Soviets again. *They will shoot me for sure.*

The camp hummed with activity. More refugees lined up at the gates, GIs hammered together structures to house them, trucks and jeeps came and went, children ran and their parents moved like tides, pestering every officer they could find for information.

In the park near the parish hall, a small boy climbed an oak tree while four adults sat in the shade beneath it. As he got closer, Maurice realized they were speaking Ukrainian. He squatted among them. "Good morning!" he said in Ukrainian, forcing a cheer he did not feel. "Where are you from?"

Two middle-aged men, one old woman and a girl who was probably twenty but looked older stared at him, wary. "Poland," said one of the men, a small, thin man with a pointy chin and nose, close-set eyes and heavy dark eyebrows. His workman's cap had a hole in the top, the cuffs of his jacket were badly frayed and his pants were stained and torn. He chewed bread slowly.

"What a coincidence—so was my mother."

"It's not such a coincidence," said the man. "Half the people here are from Poland."

"Where are you from?" the young woman asked. She had limp light brown hair that looked as if she had cut it short herself. She wore men's clothes, as tattered and stained as her companion's.

"Montreal. In Canada," he answered. The group looked at him, questions in their eyes, then at each other and then back at him again.

"What are you doing here?" asked the first man with the pointy chin.

Maurice sighed. He hoped that the story he had come up with in the weeks since he had left Berlin would sound believable. "I was in the army and got captured by the Germans. I escaped before the end of the war, and I haven't been able to find my unit since." The Ukrainians' eyes grew wide when he mentioned escaping. The men exchanged a look and leaned closer. "The trouble is, I'm not an official 'displaced person' according to the Americans here. So they won't let me stay here."

The group looked at Maurice for a long moment, then at each other. Finally, the man with the pointy chin asked him his name and began telling him their story.

They were the Tkacz family, from a farming community outside L'viv. He was Jaroslav, and the younger man was his son, Basil. The old lady, Perenye, was his aunt. Lana was her daughter and Jaroslav's niece. In 1941, the Germans had confiscated their farm and forced them to work on it to feed the *Wehrmacht*. When the Red Army advanced into western Ukraine in 1944, the Germans loaded them and thousands of other slaves onto trains and sent them west. "They put us in a factory near Munich, making bullets," Lana, the young woman, said. "We worked from dawn to dusk, and only stopped because they turned out all the lights at night."

"Because of the bombing," said Jaroslav. "They had blackouts to try to hide from the bombers. The Americans and the English bombed nearly every night."

"A bomb hit the factory," said the old woman, Perenye.

"That's how we got away," Lana continued. "One night, we heard the airplanes coming closer, closer, closer. Then we heard the explosions, the bombs coming closer. And then one hit, *boom!* and blasted a big hole in the wall of our barracks."

"Our prison, you mean," said Jaroslav.

"Yes. The bomb killed a lot of the guards and we could run away from there."

"It killed prisoners, too," said Jaroslav.

"Do you smell smoke?" said the younger man, Basil.

They saw a black cloud billowing out of a window of the parish hall. Maurice and Basil ran toward the half-open rear door.

The back half of the hall was a large kitchen, which the GIs had taken over for the enlisted men's mess. Maurice and Basil charged in to see smoke rising from a frypan on one of three stoves. No one else was around.

Maurice pulled his cuff over his hand and slid the pan off the stove onto a table, letting go before it could hurt him. Basil propped the door open and then pushed the windows wider, and the smoke gradually cleared. "What kind of idiot leaves a frypan on a hot stove to burn?" he wondered.

"I can't understand why there's no one in an army kitchen," said Maurice. The frypan was not the only thing that was hot. Pots bubbled furiously on all three stoves. The bottom of the frypan was black, and dark chunks smouldered. "I think they were frying sliced potatoes."

He ladled the hash browns that were not too burned into a metal bowl, then threw the burnt pieces out the door. Immediately, dogs appeared and gobbled them down, panting out the heat from the burned tubers.

Beside the stove was a big bowl of raw potato chunks and another tub of fat. Basil gobbled down two pieces of potato, but Maurice pushed him away before he could take more. Maurice spooned a generous helping of fat into the frypan, set it back on the stove and when the lard had melted, dumped in a helping of potatoes. He was stirring the hash browns and humming when a soldier in a green undershirt, long white apron and white hat came in. "Who the hell are you two?" He did not look more than 18 years old.

Maurice turned around slowly and smiled a little. "Don't you know never to leave a fry pan unwatched?" he asked in his best English. Then he returned his attention to the pan.

"I—I just stepped outside for a minute ..." the soldier babbled. "What do you know about a mess kitchen?"

"I know how to cook."

The soldier hesitated, then nodded. "Okay, then. You keep at them hash browns. And you," he pointed at Basil, "can peel more 'taters." He gave them each a long apron and a hair net. "Standing orders. If you work in a kitchen, you gotta keep your hair outta the food."

Basil just looked at the young soldier. "I don't think he speaks English," Maurice said. He translated. Basil nodded, picked up a knife and went to work on a huge pile of potatoes.

Basil was tall with long, thin legs, arms and fingers. Younger than Jaroslav, he might have been handsome, but now his black hair was thin and limp and dirty. Crescents as dark as bruises hung under his eyes and a scar stood out angry and red across his neck. Maurice wondered how he had escaped a hanging. But in the kitchen, his long fingers moved quickly, efficiently stripping the peel off a potato and moving to the next one.

Maurice was finishing the third batch of hash browns and the GI cook was stirring a soup pot when into the kitchen came the lieutenant that had told Maurice he could not stay. "What's going on here, sergeant? Why are these two civilians in the kitchen?"

The sergeant stood tall and saluted. "I saw 'em hangin' around the back door, lookin' hungry," he said smoothly. "I figgered it'd be better to put 'em to work than lettin' 'em steal food. 'Sides, we're s'posed to give work to the dee-pees when we can, ain't we? En I'm short-handed since Willy got hurt."

The lieutenant looked confused, then exasperated. Finally, he shook his head. "Fine. Keep an eye on them, get some use out of them, and after cleanup, I want to see all three of you in my office."

The GI cook saluted again. When the kitchen door closed behind the lieutenant, the cook thumbed his nose. "War's over," he said to Maurice. "I don't see why we gotta still follow all these goddamn army procedures. I'm Leo. Corporal Zyskowski. What's your name, mac?"

"No, not 'Mac.' Maurice. And this is Basil. Or you can call him 'William.'"

"No, we already got a Willy. Dumb son-of-a-bitch burned his hand and now he can't work in a kitchen. Prob'ly did it on purpose. So you," he pointed a chin at Basil, "Will just be plain 'Basil.'"

The three men bustled around the kitchen, with Maurice and Basil helping wherever Corporal Zyskowski directed them. When the GIs filed into the mess, Maurice and Basil ladled mashed potatoes onto plates. None of the men even noticed the newcomers.

After cleanup, Maurice, Basil and Leo went to a house near the camp. It was a handsome home that had once belonged to a wealthy German, with a neat front porch and nearly clean windows. Every line of the building was perfectly straight, and any dirt or scuff marks on the floors and walls was new, the fault of careless American soldiers.

The lieutenant was sitting in the parlour, on a formal and very German-looking chair. Sitting at a table on a wooden chair was another corporal, in full uniform. He looked even younger than Leo. He held a pencil in one hand and a ledger was spread on the table in front of him.

Leo saluted, and Maurice thought it was a little too stiff and formal, bordering on ironic. "Corporal Zyskowski reporting as ordered, Lieutenant Gardner." The other corporal scribbled on the ledger and Lieutenant Gardner returned Corporal Zyskowski's salute without rising. "So, who are these two?"

"This is Maurice, and this is Basil, sir," Zyskowski answered.

"Do they have last names?"

"Bury," Maurice volunteered. "I am Maurice Bury."

"Yes, I remember you. I told you you're not eligible to stay here. What about the other one?"

"He's Tkacz. He doesn't speak English," said Maurice.

"Catch?" asked the corporal at the table.

"Tkacz," Maurice repeated.

"T-cats?" said the corporal.

"T-K-A-C-Z."

"'Zed'? What's a 'zed'?"

"'Zee,'" Maurice answered.

"They're both real good workers and know their way around a kitchen, Lieutenant," Leo said, still standing at attention.

Lieutenant Gardner looked at the two men, lips pursed. Finally, he nodded. "Very well, Corporal," he turned to his secretary. "Give them both D.P. cards and record them as being on K.P. duty. We'll pay them out of the U.N. funds."

Pay us? Maurice thought. He began to breathe a little faster.

The corporal at the table shuffled some papers, asked Maurice for the spelling of Basil's name again. He scribbled with his pen and handed each of them a small piece of white cardboard.

Maurice translated for Basil: "Allied Expeditionary Force, D.P. Index Card," he read. "'D.P. for 'displaced person.' That, across the card, says 'Not a pass.' That means you cannot use it to go out of the camp. It has your name here, in Western script. There was also a serial number on the front, beside big, bold letters "GB."

He turned the card over and translated the back for Basil. "'Keep this card at all times to assist your safe return home. The Registration Number and your name identify you and your Registration Record.'"

"I already have one of these."

"Keep both. You never know when you'll need an extra one."

"You need to sign them," said the corporal. He held out a fountain pen.

Basil took it first and signed his name in Cyrillic script on the front.

Maurice looked at his: the corporal had spelled his name *BURE MORITZ.*

I guess that's what I sound like to American ears. He took the fountain pen, and only when he finished signing the card did he realize he had also signed using Cyrillic script.

The lieutenant dismissed them and they went back to the camp in the late-setting June sun. "Don't worry, Morrie," Leo said when Maurice showed him his D.P. card. "The army spelled my name wrong, too. To them, I'm 'Lytkowski.' But I still get paid."

Maurice's life took on a new pattern then. He stayed in the U.S. Army-issued tent with the Tkaczes at night, and rose with the early June sunrise to go to the kitchen for what the Americans called "K.P."—kitchen duty. He and Basil peeled potatoes and fried them, chopped vegetables, stirred pots, brought in pails of water, swept and scrubbed and fetched things for Corporal Leo Zyskowski or Lytkowski. They ate after serving the meals to the soldiers and officers, and in the evening, Basil brought some of the leftovers to the other members of his family. "Don't worry about it," Zyskowski said. "The army throws all that out, anyway."

During the supper preparation on their third day of K.P., Zyskowski put eight huge hams on the counter. With a long, thin knife he started slicing off the outer layer of fat and pushed great white slices to the side of the counter.

Maurice's stomach rumbled. "What are you going to do with that?" he asked.

"Just throw it out," the cook shrugged. "The boys don't eat it, anyway."

"Well, let us take it. Our people love that."

The cook shrugged and waved his hand.

Maurice and Basil ran to the Tkaczes' tent, thinking only of not dropping the ham fat. Jaroslav was trying to wash his clothes in a leaky wooden bucket. "What the hell do you look so happy for?"

"Shenka, Jaroslav! Ham!" Maurice could barely keep from shouting, but did not want to start a stampede. Every refugee was hungry.

Jaroslav's eyes grew wide. He grabbed one of the fattest pieces from Basil and stuffed it in his mouth.

"Oh, it's been so long since I had any ham, or anything good to eat!" Jaroslav stuck his tongue out a few times because he had gotten dirty laundry water on the ham. He looked intently at his nephew. "Where did you get it?"

Maurice bent close, careful to keep the rest of the ham fat out of Jaroslav's reach. "The Americans just throw it away!"

"Throw it away!"

"In the garbage. The cook said we could have it. He didn't care."

Jaroslav shook his head. "These cowboys don't know what's good. We can make *skvarke*. Can you get any onions?"

Maurice shook his head. "Let's not push our luck, Jaroslav."

Basil stoked up the fire in front of the tent and set up a fry pan. Maurice cut up the ham fat into tiny chunks and dropped them in. Lana and Perenye brought some bread and salt they had scavenged from somewhere and they dipped chunks of stale bread into the melting ham fat. It wasn't very good, with stale bread and no seasoning other than a little salt, but it reminded Maurice of home. He began to cry. Basil saw the tears on his cheeks and nodded. He was weeping, too.

The Americans' garbage became the salvation of a growing number of D.P.s. At the end of each day, Basil and Maurice took buckets of discarded ends of roasts and hams, vegetables, loaves and other food and distributed it to hungry refugees. At first, it was just the tents near them; then, other Ukrainians; then more people from, it seemed, every part of Europe.

It's getting out of control, Maurice thought a week later. Every time he came back to his tent, there was a crowd of people looking at him hopefully. Every day, the crowd got bigger, but he never had more food. It was getting harder and harder to ration the food out fairly, and no one was getting enough. And rather than feeling better, Maurice started to feel more and more pressured, more like he was surrounded by enemies than friends. *It's not much better than the POW camp*, he thought.

No, that's not true. There is enough food here, and no one is going to shoot us for leaving

"Zyskowski. That is Polish name?" Maurice asked in English one day.

"Yah. Ma and Pop came to Milwaukee from Poland," Zyskowski answered as he set several cabbages on the counter.

"I have an idea for something special," said Maurice. "How would you like I'll make you a special recipe of my mother's?"

"What do you have in mind?"

"Cabbage rolls."

The corporal smiled slowly and widely. "I don't believe it! My ma makes great cabbage rolls! Where the hell are you really from?"

"Montreal. But my mother is from ... Poland." It had been Poland when she was born there. Maurice hoped again that his mother and sister were all right, and also that his face did not betray his feelings.

"I haven't had any Polish cooking since I joined the goddamn army. If you know how to make good gołąbki, be my guest. How many cabbages do you want?"

Maurice picked up the best-looking one. "Just this. Do you have any rice?"

The sergeant happily brought Maurice everything he asked for: salt, butter, pepper (which Maurice had not seen since before the war), onions. Maurice put a big pot on to boil and began chopping onions. As the cabbage leaves gradually separated from the head in the boiling water, he fried the onions and started cooking the rice.

Making a pot of cabbage rolls takes hours. Maurice hummed to himself as he fried the onions with some leftover hamburger from the previous day's meal, and he had to keep himself from singing as he spooned the rice and onions onto softened cabbage leaves and rolled them closed. He put them into an iron pot, put the pot in the wood oven, stoked up the fire a little...and waited.

Just before the GIs' lunch, he filled a plate with cabbage rolls, topped them with a spoonful of fried onions and presented it to Corporal Zyskowski. The army cook smacked his lips and dug in, chomping down huge mouthfuls. "Oh, Morrie! Geez, these are almost as good as Ma's!" He swallowed and shoveled in another huge bite. "Ya know, if you have a sister and she has this recipe, tell her I'll marry her!"

Maurice took a small pot for the Tkaczes and himself, but he knew it would only be enough for a taste for each of them. He felt happy, at least a little, for pleasing Zyskowski. But cabbage rolls were not such a hit with the officers.

"What is this?" said Lieutenant Gardner.

"Morrie there made a special recipe from his ma," said the sergeant. "It's good—"

"Get this away from me and bring me some decent American food!"

The new pattern did not last long. In early July, orders came from somewhere to close down the Ingolstadt camp. "We're moving south, to Austria," Lieutenant Gardner said. "All the D.P.s will move to a new camp in Landeck, Austria."

On the last day in Ingolstadt, July 7, 1945, Lieutenant Gardner surprised Maurice with a letter typed on tissue-thin, army-issued paper.

Recen. Co. 692 T.D.Bn.
July 7, 1945

To whom it may concerns:

     The following two men, Maurice Bury, and Tkacz Bazyli , have been working for us as K.P.s for the last xxxxx month, and we have found there work to be very satisfactory.
We recommend them very highly.

Signed,
John Gardner
1st Lt. F.A.
commanding

Racen. Co. 692 T.D.Bn.
July 7, 1945.

To whom it may concerns:

The following two men, Maurice Bury, and Tkacz Bazyli , have been working for us as K. P.s for the last xxxxx month, and we have found there work to be very satisfactory.

We recommend them very highly.

signed. *John W. Gardner*
John Gardner
1st Lt. F.A.
commanding

"It's a letter of reference," Corporal Zyskowski said. "I asked him to write it. It'll help you get work."

Maurice could not think of anything better to say than "Thank you."

As they walked away, Basil said to Maurice, "They got my name backwards. 'Tkacz Bazyli'?"

"I thought you couldn't speak English."

"That's what I wanted them to think."

Maurice waved the letter under Basil's nose. "Still want that?"

The GIs herded the refugees out of the camp to the train station. Clinging to the few possessions they had, they climbed onto passenger and freight cars. As the train lurched forward and began to roll out of the station, Maurice saw several of the women crying.

"Do you think the Americans are sending us back to the Russians?" Lana asked, her eyes wide. Maurice saw her hands trembling. Behind her, her grandmother wept with her hands over her face.

"The Americans wouldn't give in to the Communists so easily," Jaroslav said. "The commandant said we're going to Tyrol. I hear the French are running the D.P. camps in Tyrol."

"You think we're going there?" Lana asked.

"Why not?"

"The Russians are taking all the Ukrainians back. They took a whole regiment of Cossacks that were fighting for the Germans. Sent them to Siberia," Basil growled.

"We're with the Americans."

"The Americans agreed to hand over any 'Soviet citizens.' Something called the Yalta Agreement," Basil answered. "They're supposed to send all the Ukrainians to the U.S.S.R." He turned to Maurice. "If you want to go to Canada, don't tell anyone you're Ukrainian."

The train crawled slowly up spectacular mountain ranges, through a high pass and then along switchbacks.

Waterfalls sparkled over the bluest lakes Maurice had ever seen as they traversed Tyrol, Austria toward Landeck.

But none of the Poles or Ukrainians could appreciate it. They all dreaded being sent east to Soviet-occupied territories.

D.T.P. 148 Camp Landeck

Landeck, Austria, 1945 – 1946

Another soup line, Maurice thought, shivering in the winter cold. *At least this time, I have a bowl.* He absently tapped it against his thigh, thinking of his mother.

The United Nations Humanitarian Relief Agency had taken a German army base in Landeck, in North Tyrol in Austria, and turned it into a refugee camp more than twice as big as Kufstein. Clapboard buildings, most with sloping roofs like lean-tos, and tents sprawled for what looked like a mile. Behind the town, green-covered mountains rose to snow-covered peaks. Trucks drove in and out of the gates continually, bringing food and other supplies, taking refugees back to their homes, or to whatever was left of their towns and villages. The French were nominally in charge, but the guards at the gates and the cooks in the kitchen were from the U.S. Army. Volunteers from the U.S. and Canada doled out food and blankets, and American medics and nurses gave pills and needles.

Maurice heard a dozen languages just walking between the barracks: the twangy English of the American GIs,

French, German, Italian, Russian, Czech, Polish, Latvian, others he could not identify—and even Ukrainian. From the lineup, he idly watched a man playing an accordion in front of a barracks building. A small crowd had gathered around him, including a young American officer. Behind the barracks, the snowy Alps seemed to protect the peace of the place, like a high wall against chaos.

Beside the accordionist, a young mother held her little boy by the hand. *How are you, Mama? This war is over, yet I still cannot see my mother.*

Fucking communists.

He had offered to work in the kitchen again, but the American lieutenant in charge had just shaken his head with no explanation. So Maurice spent his first few days looking for ways to fill up the day, when he wasn't writing and posting letters to his father in Montreal, or to various Ukrainian and Canadian organizations. He needed more than just a Canadian birth certificate to travel home: he needed two different permits from the occupying forces in Austria, plus money to buy a ticket.

"Maurice Bury!" boomed out behind him as someone slapped his shoulder. Maurice sprang forward, dropping his soup bowl into the mud. He started to run, but looked over his shoulder to see ...

Ivan Babiak, his neighbour from Nastasiv in what was once eastern Poland and after Stalin's re-drawing of the borders was now in the Ukrainian Soviet Socialist Republic.

"Easy, Maurice, easy!" Ivan laughed.

Ivan. Not the NKVD. Not the Communists. Maurice straightened. His mind whirled. Not the Communists, he thought over and over. "Ivan," he croaked. "How the hell did you find me here?"

Ivan looked mystified. "I wasn't looking for you, believe me. I was as surprised as you—well, not quite as surprised. I didn't shit my pants, at least!" He laughed again.

Maurice picked up his soup-bowl and tried to wipe the dirt off it. Moving forward to keep his place in line, he said

"Never sneak up on a person like that!" He stopped himself from saying "I thought you were the NKVD."

"We're heading west, away from the commies," Ivan said.

"We?"

Ivan pointed into the crowd behind him. "My brother and my cousin are with me."

"How did you get out of Ukraine?"

Ivan shrugged. "When we heard the fighting was over, we piled stuff in a wagon and cut across fields at night. We managed to stay away from the Reds by hiding during the day and moving only at night. We nearly made it to the Swiss border, and then we saw a Red Army camp there. We turned back and followed a bunch of other people here. What about you? I thought the army took you. That's what people said in the village."

Maurice ignored that. "What about the rest of your family?"

Ivan looked down. "We're going to Canada, and when we get settled, we'll bring them over. Come on, they'll love seeing you. One thing, though. Don't mention Michael's mother."

"Why not?"

"The communists took her."

"Took her where? Why?" Maurice didn't feel horror, though. He had seen too much to be horrified.

"They wanted to draft Michael, but he hid in the country. So the Reds shipped his mother to the gulag. Siberia."

"No!"

"Yes. There was nothing we could do. After they took her, the rest of us took off."

I've left my mother behind, too, Maurice thought. *Neither of us had a choice.*

"So, Maurice, how did you get here? Weren't you in the army? This is a civilian camp!"

"Shut up about the army, will you?" Maurice growled. "I'm a civilian, just like you. Look—don't you see 'Canada' on my cap?"

Ivan looked at Maurice's hat. "Where did you get that?"

"Listen to me, Ivan, keep your voice down. Better yet, don't speak Ukrainian."

"Why not?"

"Have you heard of the Yalta Conference? All citizens of the Soviet Union are going to be sent back there. Whether they want to go or not. So speak Polish or German."

"I can't speak German."

"Then stay with Polish." It was still risky. All displaced persons were supposed to be returned to the country of their birth. Stalin had shifted Poland's borders to the West, so that Ternopyl and L'viv, within Polish borders before the war, would now be within the Ukrainian Soviet Socialist Republic. Ukrainians had dreamt of united Ukraine, but under Stalin, it would be a nightmare. They all knew of the famine that Stalin had engineered in Ukraine in 1933, by taking all the harvest out of the country. Millions had starved to death, collapsing in the streets.

As the line moved up, Ivan chatted on in Polish. Maurice just nodded and grunted replies, trying hard not to look like he was scanning the camp for NKVD or Red Army soldiers. He didn't notice when a Red Cross volunteer ladled soup into his bowl, and Ivan had to take a piece of bread for him.

Ivan carried two bowls. Walking carefully so as not to spill his soup, he led Maurice to a small wagon where his brother and cousin waited. They were both short and stocky like him, and like him wore torn and battered clothing. Maurice glanced into the wagon, which held cloth bags with a few extra clothes, some basic tools, a ball of twine, a fry pan and a bandura. Twine secured a wooden box to the side of the wagon.

Pathetic. Why bother with the wagon at all?

"Maurice Bury!" said Michael, the youngest Babiak, the one they usually called Mihach. "I don't believe it!" He smiled broadly. Mihach always had such white teeth, Maurice remembered and ran his tongue over his own still-tender gums.

"Keep it down, and don't say my name out loud anymore!" Maurice growled.

"He's afraid of the commies," said Ivan, not smiling.

"You should be, too," said Maurice. Mihach turned away to keep from crying.

"What happened to your teeth, Maurice?" asked Slawko, Ivan's brother.

"Accident," he muttered. He did not want to risk telling them about how his own rifle butt had smashed out some of his front teeth. He didn't think the Babiaks would knowingly betray him, but he knew he was safer if no one knew that he had walked away from the Red Army once the fighting was over.

He decided to stay away from the Babiaks, and other Ukrainians as much as possible. He slurped his lukewarm soup, popped the crust of bread in his mouth and said "See you later," then went back to the wooden barracks the American soldiers had built for D.P.s. The haste of the construction was plain in gaps between the wallboards and the way every door stuck.

It's too dangerous to be a Ukrainian today, he thought. *As usual.*

The Ukrainian refugees in Landeck, "displaced persons," filled their days playing music, building new barracks or talking among their countrymen, enquiring about their friends and families. Most refused the directives to return to the USSR, especially the thousands of teachers, lawyers, engineers, physicians and university students. They simply refused to board trains and trucks headed eastward, and instead wrote letters applying to emigrate to the United

States, Canada, Australia, Britain, France, even Brazil and Argentina.

Many managed to get authorization to emigrate to those countries. In the meantime, the thousands of Ukrainians still in the camps in the British, American and French-occupied zones in Germany and Austria organized elementary and high schools. They organized churches, orchestras and choirs, performed plays and concerns. They set up libraries and published thousands of periodicals and books.

And being Ukrainians, they argued about politics, religion and whether the Bandera or Melnyk factions of the Ukrainian National Organization was the legitimate government of a theoretical free Ukraine.

American and French doctors and nurses treated wounds, colds, flus and malnutrition. Civilian workers who spoke English, French or, occasionally, German, gave out clothes, food, towels, soap and dozens of other supplies that people needed every day.

For Maurice, time dragged. Wanting to stay away from the Ukrainians, he had little opportunity for social interaction, especially since Ukrainians made up a greater proportion of the population of the Landeck camp. Maurice missed the conversations he was used to and ached to join in the debates over politics. But it was too dangerous for anyone to find out that he had been part of the Red Army that took Berlin.

With little else to occupy his mind, he worried about his mother. She couldn't know whether he was alive or dead. For that matter, he had no idea whether she was still alive, or what the communists might have done to her. Maurice spent the next few days avoiding the Babiaks and other Ukrainians. He felt nervous all the time and kept looking to the camp gates for trucks with a red star.

The summer and fall passed. Winter was hard in the camp. The inhabitants worked to improve the insulation of the barracks and secure more fuel. American, French and other

United Nations officials doled out what clothing and other supplies they could, but existence in the camp was miserable.

Maurice finally gave up isolating himself from the other Ukrainians and joined in the efforts to improve living conditions. He went out of the camp with the Babiaks to search for food and odd jobs for the local Austrian inhabitants.

One day, they woke to find the countryside covered in fresh snow. Maurice and the Babiaks wandered out, looking for scrap wood to burn.

Mihach was acting strangely. He seemed filled with nervous energy, jumpy, smiling without reason. He looked at his cousins and Maurice as if he were about to tell them something, but then turned away.

"For god's sake, Mihach, what is it?" Ivan demanded, but Mihach just shook his head.

When they reached the base of a disused ski resort on the edge of town, Mihach reached into his coat pocket and pulled out an old, battered camera. Grinning, he brandished it for his companions.

"Where did you get that?" Ivan asked.

"A farmer I cut some wood for gave it to me," he answered. "He said he had no money, but he gave me this camera. It even has film in it."

"Why didn't you take some of the firewood as payment?" Ivan asked.

"He said he needed all of it for his family," Mihach said. "But I wanted the camera, anyway." He stepped back from them and squinted through the viewfinder. "Smile!"

"Have you ever used a camera, Mihach?" Maurice asked.

"No, but it can't be hard. The farmer showed me. You look through here, then push this button." They heard the shutter click. Mihach lowered the camera and thumbed a small wheel on the top. "Now, you wind the film to the next ... um, picture." He raised the camera again. "Come on, boys, do something interesting."

Ivan and Slawko looked at each other. Maurice picked up a handful of snow and threw it at Ivan, smacking him in the chest. "Hey!" he said, but Maurice threw another snowball.

Soon, the brothers and Maurice were chasing each other across the field. Ivan threw a snowball and Maurice tackled him, pushing him onto the field.

"Hold it!" said Mihach. "That's perfect. Slawko, get in there, too."

Maurice picked up another handful of snow as he reclined against the sprawling Ivan. Slawko knelt behind them and grinned at the camera, and Mihach snapped the shot.

On a sunny day, Maurice leaned against the wall of a building near the camp's main gate, huddling against the wind sweeping down from the mountains. He heard voices and snapped his head up. *Did I just hear Russian?*

Then he saw what he had dreaded most: a Studebaker truck, its back covered in canvas that bore a red star, idled just inside the gate. Red Army. They've come for me.

On the passenger side running board, a young man in a Soviet commissar's uniform argued with a U.S. sergeant standing on the ground in front of the truck. Three other GIs stood in the mud around the truck, holding rifles across their chests. They looked nervous, and so did the driver, but the sergeant seemed relaxed. "Take me to the commandant of this camp!" the commissar on the running board shouted in Russian.

"Take it easy, Eye-van," said the sergeant in lazy, stretched English vowels. He had black hair under his cap, a blunt nose and thin lips. Even though he was clean-shaven, his dark stubble was already visible in the morning. "Now you just back up your Russkie truck back through those gates and wait a spell."

"Out of the way!" the commissar shouted, still in Russian, sweeping his arm across the field. There was no way anyone could misunderstand what he wanted. He pointed into the camp. "We are coming to see the commandant and to find deserters!"

Maurice felt cold.

But the sergeant just shook his head. "You ain't comin' another inch into this here camp," he drawled. He stepped closer to the front of the truck, then put his hand on the grille as if he were going to push it out the gate. "Now back up."

"Out of the way!" the commissar shouted.

"Speak English, Russkie!" the sergeant snapped. "Now get the hell out of here before I order my men to fire!" The soldiers around the truck brought their rifles to their shoulders.

The commissar's eyes narrowed, but he did not reply. He snarled an order at the driver, then jumped to the ground, slamming the truck's door. The truck backed out, gears grinding, onto the road just outside the gates. The commissar stepped closer to the sergeant. "Take me to your commander," he ordered.

The American stepped until his nose nearly touched the commissar's. "I told you to speak English if you want somethin'," he drawled. "Now, turn around and walk out of here while you still can walk on your own."

A young American lieutenant strode across the camp toward the truck. "What's going on here, Sergeant Brown?"

Without moving from the commissar's face, the sergeant said "Eye-van here wants to drive his commie-painted Studebaker into the camp with a buncha Red riflemen. I told him no."

"What do you want, mister?" the officer asked the commissar.

The commissar turned to the lieutenant. "You are not the commandant of this facility! I demand to see the man in charge!" he said in Russian.

"Don't you speak English?" the lieutenant asked. He looked around. "Can anyone here interpret?"

Opportunity overcame fear in Maurice. He stepped forward and saluted the lieutenant. "I can interpret, lieutenant," he said, trying very hard to speak English with as much of an American accent as he could.

The American lieutenant and the sergeant turned to him. "Huh?" the lieutenant said. "Who are you?"

"My name is Maurice Bury. I can speak Russian and English. I can translate for you."

The Americans still looked confused. Maurice fought down the panic that was telling him to run as fast and as far as he could. "Where are you from?" the lieutenant asked.

"Canada." That particular truth was safest, he knew. But he still felt like he was making a huge mistake.

"Huh. And what're you doin' here, Bury?" the lieutenant demanded.

"My family came to Poland when I was a boy."

"So, you're a Polish national?"

"No, I'm Canadian." Maurice thought of Ivan Babiak's mother, sentenced to Siberia when her son hid from the army. *Don't say anything about Poland or Ukraine. Returning to the USSR is a death sentence. The Red Army considers you a deserter.*

"Okay, Bury, tell me what the commissar wants," said the American lieutenant.

"He wants to see the commandant of the camp," Maurice answered.

"Geez, Bury's English ain't much better'n my Russkie," said Sergeant Brown. "He must be from the French part'a Canada."

"Yes!" said Maurice, relieved that they believed his story. *Sometimes, the truth serves.* "Montreal."

"Great. That's all we need. A Frog to translate Russkie to English," the sergeant muttered.

The lieutenant ignored that. "Why does he want to see the commandant?"

Maurice turned to the commissar, who was stewing in front of the gate. "Why do you want to see the commandant," he asked in what he hoped sounded like French-accented Russian.

The commissar looked suspicious for a second, then answered "We need to see the names of the internees."

"They're not internees in this camp," Maurice argued. "They're refugees. Why do you need to see the lists?"

"We are looking for criminals and deserters. Now stop this delaying!"

Maurice turned back to the lieutenant. "They want to see the names of everyone in the camp and round up all the Russians and anyone from the Soviet Union. They want to take them back."

"No way!" exclaimed the sergeant. "Lieutenant, tell Eye-van there to beat it!"

"That's enough, Sergeant," said the lieutenant. "Bury, tell the commissar to back the truck out of the gate. He can come with me to the commandant's office."

"Are you sure?" Maurice asked.

"Are you questioning me?" the lieutenant snapped. "Do as you're told, or I'll find someone else to translate. Someone who can speak better English." He turned on his heel and strode toward the commandant's quarters. The sergeant gestured at the commissar, who followed, with Maurice trotting behind.

What have I done? Maurice asked himself. The lieutenant stomped up the wooden steps, but a guard would let neither him nor the Russian commissar enter. Then again, what would any other translator have done? At least he was close to whatever would happen, he told himself. He would have the earliest warning if anything happened—if the Russians were about to round up deserters like himself.

He folded his arms so no one could see his hands shaking. *Why am I so scared? I've been in worse danger before. Many times.*

But he had never been so close to freedom before.

The commandant's door opened and a voice barked a command he did not understand. One of the guards motioned him and the commissar inside.

The office was dim after the morning sunlight. It was plain; a corporal sat behind a small metal desk that held a radio, a telephone and a small pile of papers. A short, thin man with wire-rim glasses, he gestured them through another door behind him. In the inner office, the commandant sat behind a battered wooden desk. A little sign on the edge of the desk read "Lt. Col. Whitney-Coates, Commandant."

"That the translator?" Commandant Whitney-Coates asked.

"Yes, sir," said the lieutenant.

"Okay, translator, tell the commissar that we've checked the records. There are no refugees here from the Soviet

Union, nor are there any deserters from the Red Army. If we find any, we will be sure to contact the appropriate United Nations authorities."

Maurice had a little trouble understanding the commandant's formal speech, but he translated the meaning to the commissar. He could tell the Russian didn't believe it.

"I demand to see the lists of names of all the internees," the commissar said, calmly and formally.

"They are not 'internees,'" Maurice repeated. He relayed the demand to the Americans, who frowned even more deeply.

"Tell comrade ... what was his name?"

"I am comrade Commissar Igor Maksov," he said in heavily accented English. *Damn*, thought Maurice. *He speaks some English.*

"Well, comrade commissar, our records are none of your business. I tell you, we have no citizens of the Soviet Union here. Translator, tell him."

Maurice repeated the commandant's words.

"If true, no reason to hide records," said Maksov in English. *Why hadn't he just spoken English at the gate?* Maurice wondered.

"That will not be necessary, commissar," the commandant said. "Now, you are dismissed." He stood.

Maksov did not move. "I not military. Not under military command. I poleetical."

The lieutenant had had enough. He took Maksov by the arm and pulled him out of the commandant's office, then out of the building. "Well, this camp is under military command right now, Ee-gor. Now go on, back to wherever your base is, and we'll keep you informed through regular channels."

The commandant followed them out the door and stood at the top of the steps to his office shed, watching the lieutenant's actions intently but not interfering.

Outside, Maksov shook himself free of the lieutenant's grip, straightened his uniform and marched through the gates to his truck without a look back. Only when he stood on the running board did he glare at the commandant. Maurice heard him bark an order at the driver. With grinding gears and swirling dust, the truck roared down the road.

"He'll be back before long, sir," said the lieutenant.

"We're ready," answered the commandant. He came down the steps to look at Maurice. "What's your name, interpreter?"

Commandant Whitney-Coates was not a tall man, and his hair was receding over his forehead. His brown U.S. Army uniform was immaculate, the creases in his pants sharp as bayonets. He looked up into Maurice's eyes. Maurice hoped he saw some kindness in the commandant's eyes. "I am Maurice Bury, Canadian citizen," he said.

"Canadian, huh?" The commandant did not look like he believed him.

"He's French, sir," the sergeant from the gate spoke up, surprising Maurice. "From Montreal. You know, Queebeck. They're all French over there. That's why he talks funny."

The commandant nodded. "You don't sound French. But that doesn't matter. What languages do you speak, Mr. Bury?"

"English, German, Russian, Polish," he replied, hesitating before he added, "and Ukrainian."

"But not French?"

Maurice nearly choked. "Oh, yes ... of course. I did not think that would be much use here." Maurice hoped the commandant could not see his heart pounding under his shirt.

"Well, the French are nominally in charge of this camp. Not that I ever see one of them around here, doing anything useful. Look, Bury, if you want to be useful to me, you can help me communicate with the refugees. Can you do that?"

"Yes, sir."

"Good." The commandant turned to the corporal who was his secretary. "Get him some decent clothes and put him on the roster as an official civilian interpreter attached to U.S. command. I don't want the Russkies getting their hands on him." He went back in his office.

Maurice knew that the commandant knew he wasn't French. He also realized he had been holding his breath.

"Come on, Bury," said the corporal and led him back to the outer office.

At the desk, Maurice pulled out a piece of paper from the secret pocket he had made inside his shirt, then unfolded the tattered, battered document. "You see? I am Canadian. Citizen of the Dominion of Canada."

The corporal studied the document. "Okay, so you're Canadian. But with that accent, don't think Ivan won't be trying to take you back home. The Yalta Conference says we gotta let Uncle Joe take all his people back where they came from. Doesn't matter what they want. Orders are orders." He held up a hand. "Don't worry. The colonel said he wants you here, so you'll stay here." He scribbled a note and handed it to Maurice. "Go see the quartermaster for some new clothes. They won't be a uniform, but they'll be army issue and clean. Then you can come to the enlisted men's mess for supper. Okay?"

"Thank you," said Maurice, pocketing his birth certificate and the corporal's note. He did not know what else to say.

That evening, Maurice sat at one end of a table at the side of the Americans' enlisted mess. It was the best meal he had had in months—in fact, in over a year, since before the Soviets had caught him outside his mother's house. There were huge joints of ham, and a mountain of mashed potatoes and beans. Maurice ate until he could not swallow another mouthful.

His life took on a new pattern then. He rose early and washed alongside the GIs. Then, shaved and feeling better than he had in years, went to the commandant's office. He would translate various refugees and local officials for Corporal Knight, the commandant's secretary, and occasionally, Commandant Whitney-Coates himself.

Maurice ate with the GIs, listening carefully to improve his command of English. He laughed when they did, stood when they did, and gradually grasped some of their slang. He became friends with Corporal Knight, who began to call him "Morrie."

And during a slack period in the office, when there were no pressing documents to translate for the commandant, Maurice took some spare stationery—the Americans always had much more of everything than they needed—and wrote a letter to his father.

Tato,

I am well. Other than losing a few teeth, I have been unhurt in the past year, and I am now in a safe location, working for the American army in Austria.

Returning to Canada will take some time, apparently. I need to get permission to travel within Austria and then to leave Europe for Canada. You may need to find a lawyer to get some of the necessary documents and permissions in Canada.

Please write to Mama to let her know that I am well.

Love, Maurice

He wrote the return address as "Landeck UNRRA D.P. Camp, Landeck, Austria." But he was careful to write only Mama," not "in Ukraine" or "in Ternopyl"—not to include information that would allow the Soviets to tie him to Ukraine or his stint in the Red Army. He knew they would be happy to force him back to Ukraine, and from there, Siberia or a firing squad.

Mail took weeks to travel across the ocean in the postwar chaos. Maurice had little to do but wait.

When a letter came back with a Canadian postmark, it was not from his father, but from his mother's sister, Eudora—Yevdokia in Ukrainian.

Dear Maurice,

We are so happy to learn that you are alive and well. It has been years since we heard any news from Ukraine that we could trust.

Your father and I spoke with a lawyer. He will apply to the Department of the Secretary of State for your repatriation as a native-born citizen.

This will take some time. We will have to get a copy of your birth certificate from the Province of Quebec, which will take some weeks or months. Also, you will need a sponsor who will pay your transportation costs and pledge to support you for five years.

We will do what we can to bring you home.

Do you have any news of your mother? We have not received any mail from Ukraine for years.

Love,

Evdokia.

Maurice had to wait. But now, he could keep busy, translating between the American Army, the Ukrainian and other D.P.s, and the Austrians in the town.

Resisting the USSR

Landeck, April 1946

Maurice spent over a year at Camp Landeck, where refugees—called "displaced persons" by the United Nations—streamed into the camp. Volunteers and soldiers erected more barracks and tents. Trucks brought food and other supplies from donors in the U.S., Canada, England. But there was never enough.

The commandant and officers talked about "repatriating" the refugees—sending as many back home as possible. For the refugees from Czechoslovakia, Romania, Poland, Austria and Germany, that meant hope. For the majority who had fled from Ukraine, Belorussia and Russia, from the Baltic countries and even from eastern Poland, it was pure terror.

Ukrainians began to flee the camp, heading west. A tent would disappear in the night; a corner of a barracks would be empty without any warning. Ukrainians would huddle to share rumors, without ever being sure that they had a shred of truth. "The Russians are rounding up Ukrainians all around, just loading them onto trucks. They don't even care if they're keeping families together."

"They're sending people to Siberia. Thousands at a time."

"They drove a group in a truck to the forest and shot them all. Just like in the Katyn Forest."

"That was Poland."

"The British forced the Cossacks to surrender to the Red Army, and they've shipped them all to Siberia."

"Didn't they come from Siberia?"

"Not from forced labour camps!"

"I heard that the Communists told the Americans to turn over a group of people they said had escaped from jail. The American army put them all in a truck and were driving them to Russian territory, but the driver spoke Ukrainian. His parents had emigrated to America. When he heard the prisoners' cries, he let them all go."

"When did this happen? Where?" Everyone wanted to know who this Ukrainian-American GI was. Everyone wanted to be in his care. The rumour-spreader could only shrug.

One dark, wet morning in April, Maurice arrived at the commandant's office just before two officers, one in a splendid French uniform, the other in the brown uniform with red accents of a Soviet political officer. Heart hammering, Maurice followed them into the commandant's office.

"Wait outside, Bury," said Corporal Knight, the commandant's secretary. "These officers speak English." Maurice saw the smug look on the Russian's face as he took out papers from a leather satchel. Then the door closed.

Maurice walked outside, but his knees would not hold him up past the porch. He sat on the steps, staring at a French-made staff car with U.N. markings on the fenders.

A group of Ukrainian men and some women gathered around the commandant's office. They saw the car in front. One man wearing a battered hat shouted "We won't go back to Russia!"

The crowd repeated him, and it turned into a chant. "We won't go back! We won't go back!"

A woman screamed "Don't send us back to slavery."

Sergeant Brown led a squadron of riflemen between the crowd and the steps of the office. At an order from Brown, they turned and faced the crowd but did not ready their weapons.

Maurice did not know how long the impromptu protest continued before the commandant's door opened again. The Soviet and the French officers came out, and Sergeant Brown's men formed a corridor to allow them to enter the staff car. The crowd's chanting changed to jeers and insults to the fleeing officers, continuing until the car was out of sight.

Maurice was still standing on the steps outside the office when Corporal Knight called him back inside. Commandant Whitney-Coates stood at the door to his office, watching the protest outside with an expression on his face that Maurice could not decipher.

Corporal Knight handed Maurice a sheet of paper with a message typed on it. "Translate this into Ukrainian and read it out to the people in Barracks 10 through 15."

Maurice had to hold the paper in both hands and brace his hands against his knees to quell their shaking enough to read the message. "All Ukrainian nationals without Allied documents will leave tomorrow at 0700 by train for L'viv and points farther east in the territory of the USSR, under terms of the Yalta Allied Conference, under authority of the United Nations Refugee Resettlement Authority. Signed, Charles Meistersheim, UNRRA and General-Commisar Pavel Orlov, USSR."

Maurice could not breathe. Corporal Knight seemed to teeter in front of his eyes, first to one side, then to the other.

Knight put his hand on Maurice's shoulder, and that steadied him. "Morrie?"

Maurice drew a shuddering breath. "You're sending them back to slavery. Many of them will be shot." He showed Knight the letter.

"Orders are orders." He smiled wryly.

"What is so fucking funny?"

Knight gave him another slip of paper. "Orders. Here are the orders you're to read to the D.P.s after the orders from the frog and the russkie."

Maurice's hands were shaking so much, he had to put the paper on the corporal's desk to read it. Then he took a deep breath and forced himself to become calm.

"When do I have to read these orders?" he asked.

"Right now."

Maurice followed Sergeant Brown and two helmeted guards to Barracks 10, one housing all Ukrainian refugees.

They passed a shed that served as the camp's post office, and Ivan Babiak came out. He ran up to Maurice to show a letter. "Look—my uncle in Montreal is sponsoring us. We have all the approvals and immigration paperwork. We're going to Canada!" He had to walk fast to keep up with Sergeant Brown and the MPs.

"When do you leave?" Maurice asked.

"We have to arrange train tickets to the Netherlands, and from there we'll take a ship to Canada. My uncle is sending money through some kind of U.N. bank, I don't know."

Maurice stopped, falling behind the soldiers. Ivan stopped, too. His smile faded when he saw Maurice's expression. "What's wrong?"

"Ivan, get out of the camp as fast as you can. Go back to your barracks and listen to the announcement that I'll make soon. And then don't delay. Don't bother with your wagon or any of that junk you brought with you. As soon as you can, get to France or Belgium or Holland and stay away from the Russians."

"What are you talking about?"

"The Russians have somehow pressured the Allies to send all the D.P.s back to the USSR. They will try to take you all back first thing tomorrow morning."

Ivan's face went white. "Where should we go?" he said, his voice hoarse.

"Another camp, preferably west of here. Show your paperwork to every official you find, but stay away from anyone from the USSR. I'll do what I can to stall things here, but go *fast*."

Ivan ran for his family's tent. Maurice ran to catch up with Sergeant Brown and the two MPs.

A mild tumult filled the barracks and piled outside it as families and individuals did the hundred things that filled refugees' days: cooking, washing, mending clothes, talking, wondering. Waiting for a letter or any word that would mean they could leave limbo.

"Attention!" Sergeant Brown said. The refugees quieted. They looked confused and worried.

Maurice's mouth was dry. He coughed before he began translating the letter into Ukrainian. Moans rose from the refugees. One woman screamed and men began shouting. "Tomorrow morning! We're not leaving. We are not Russians."

Maurice held one hand up for quiet, and then shouted out the second order from Commandant Whitney-Coates. The protests changed to cheers.

Maurice and the American soldiers walked out of the barracks, leaving a tumult behind them. One of the G.I.s remained outside the door as Brown, Maurice and the second guard went from building to building. Every time, they got the same reaction.

Maurice did not need to continue reading the orders after the third barracks. The word spread throughout the camp like a virus.

After supper, Maurice went to the camp office and typed a letter, posting it for another camp, in Kufstein, Austria—

closer to Russia but also closer to Austrian command in Vienna.

The next morning, Maurice sat with Corporal Knight in the American mess for breakfast, as usual. No one talked about the Soviets or the repatriation orders. When he came out of the main mess hall, he found the refugees milling around the camp as usual, teaching children, fixing the buildings, acting as if there had been no announcement about forced repatriation.

A train chuffed to a halt at the platform two hours late. A company of NKVD soldiers got off, rifles ready. Sergeant Brown led a company of American GIs to the platform, helmets on their heads and rifles slung over their shoulders. They spread across the platform, blocking the NKVD men. The Americans stood with their rifles ready, watching them.

General-Commisar Pavel Orlov climbed down from the train and walked between the NKVD soldiers. Commandant Whitney-Coates stepped from between the GIs.

"Where are the internees?" asked Orlov. He was a thin, bald man with three scars across his left cheek.

"They are not internees. They are displaced persons," Commandant Whitney-Coates said.

Orlov turned toward the camp. A crowd of men and women had gathered just inside the fence. They faced the Soviet soldiers, united in defiance.

"Ukrainians!" Orlov shouted. "Brothers and sisters. We are here to liberate you and return you to your homeland, to the freedom of a socialist society. We need you to help rebuild the country after this great patriotic struggle for freedom and democracy."

Maurice could have written the crowd's response to that statement.

Orlov turned to Whitney-Coates. Sergeant Brown lifted his hand, and the American company, moving as a single man, readied their rifles.

"You're not taking anyone back to the Soviet Union," Whitney-Coates said. "Get back on the train and get out of here."

"We are operating under the authority of the United Nations," Orlov said.

"As are we," said Whitney-Coates. "There is no one here eligible for repatriation to the U.S.S.R. Now, take your men out of my camp. Under the authority of the United Nations."

Sergeant Brown smiled as Orlov considered his options, then barked orders in Russian. The NKVD company shouldered their weapons and marched onto the train.

As he stepped onto the train, Orlov turned to Whitney-Coates one last time. "We'll be back."

"So will we," Whitney-Coates said.

Maurice let his breath out as the train's bell rang and stood still on the platform until the train was out of sight. He still had the orders memorized: the first, commanding the D.P.s to be ready for repatriation under orders from the UNNRA; and the second, ordering the residents of Camp Landeck to remain in their barracks in the morning. Then he went to the commandant's office and carefully typed out another letter and slipped it into the U.N. mailbag.

Transfers

May 1946

By late May, some refugees were beginning to give up. On a bright afternoon, a non-military Russian-made truck took three families from Belarus back to help rebuild their homes.

Maurice knew it was time for him to leave. Few of the refugees in the camp, and probably none of the American and French guards believed that he was from Montreal.

Then Corporal Knight handed him an envelope bearing the stamp of the United Nations Relief and Rehabilitation Administration, or UNRRA. "This came for you in today's mailbag, Morrie." The letter had been opened, following the protocol of the U.N. and the American Army to check letters sent through their postal system but addressed to non-military or U.N. personnel.

Heartbeat accelerating, Maurice unfolded the letter. It was a small piece of paper, two-thirds the size of the standard letter paper the Army used, and again, it bore the UNRRA. heading, along with a more specific designation of the author in French.

However, the text was perfectly typed in English.

"This is to certify that the U.N.R.R.A. Administration has no objection to accepting Mr. Maurice Bury, a Canadian subject, as an inhabitant of Camp Kufstein."

THE
UNITED NATIONS RELIEF AND REHABILITATION
ADMINISTRATION
DISPLACED PERSONS CENTRE KUFSTEIN

TEAM 199   YOUR REF.,   CIVIL KUFSTEIN 74
DIRECTOR: OUR REF.:   TELEPHONE: MILITARY KUFSTEIN 805
E. F. SQUADRILLE

Service des Personnes Déplacées,
Gouvernement Militaire,
KUFSTEIN.

3rd May, 1946.

This is to certify that the U.N.R.R.A. Administration
has no objection to accepting Mr. Maurice Bury, a Canadian
subject, as an inhabitant of Camp Kufstein.

E.F. Squadrille
Director, Camp Kufstein.

POSTAL ADDRESS: UNRRA TEAM 199 c/o HQ USFA APO 777 U.S. Army.
ADRESSE POSTALE: UNRRA TEAM 199 SECTEUR POSTAL 50353

It was signed by E.F. Squadrille, Director, Camp Kufstein, and stamped by the U.N.R.R.A.-D.P. Center – Kufstein."

Camp Kufstein was close to the German border, and closer to the U.S.S.R.

"You planning on leaving us, Morrie?" Knight asked. He sat behind his desk, and Maurice thought he looked a little hurt. "What's the matter? Don't you like us no more?"

"No, nothing like that ... I applied to go to Kufstein about a month ago. Now I have permission to go. But I don't know how I can arrange transportation there."

But there was one important aspect of the letter that Maurice knew was more important than permission to travel that he neither wanted nor could afford. Director Squadrille's letter, stamped with the official mark of an agency of the United Nations, acknowledged him as a "Canadian subject."

Documentation was the only weapon Maurice could use to save himself from the NKVD, and this would be a powerful addition to his arsenal.

Kufstein was about 150 kilometres, or 100 miles from Landeck. While civilian trains had been partially restored in Austria, buying a ticket required that he had permission to travel from the Allied occupying forces. If Corporal Knight' reaction was any indication, Maurice might have trouble getting those permits from Commandant Whitney-Coates.

Soon after that, a letter arrived that changed his plans.

It came in a large envelope made of heavy, almost luxurious paper with a Montreal return address. The unfolded letter inside bore a red wax notary's seal at the bottom left corner, and his Aunt Eudora's signature on the right.

C A N A D A
PROVINCE OF QUEBEC
DISTRICT OF MONTREAL
                    A F F I D A V I T

I, the undersigned, Mrs. Evdokia Babiak,business Lady,
residing and conduct the business at 1915 Centre St. Montreal, Que.
Canada, after being duly sworn in , on the Holy Gospel, before the
undersigned Commissaire of the Superiour Court, declared and say:

-       That I am a Canadian Citizen .

That Mr. Bury Maurice who was born in Canada, and who is at
Present in Austria directed by the address U.N.R.R.A. D.P.C. 188,
Camp Landeck, Turol Austria-is my cousin.
        That his sincere wish to leave Europe and establish
himself in Montreal Canada as soon as possible.

        That to give security to the Government of the Country
where he has chosen to live, to the effect that he will
have sufficient money to live independently, without being
at the charge of the Government, I, the undersigned, bind
and oblige myself to take care of my said cousin, to pay
all the transportation fees, and to provide him with -
sufficient money, for any other living expenses.

---   That my present wealth is approximately of $15.000.
                And I have signed at Montreal, Canada, this
25th day of April, 1946.

Ewdokia,

Mrs. Dora,

_____ Babiak

Sworn before me , at the City
of Montreal, Canada, on this
25th,day of April, 1946.

P.R. Rhodes
Commissaire of the Superior Court.

C A N A D A

PROVINCE OF QUEBEC

DISTRICT OF MONTREAL

A F F I D A V I T

     I, the undersigned, Mrs. Ewdokia Babiak, business Lady, residing and conduct the business at 1915 Centre St. Montreal, Que. Canada, after being duly sworn in , on the Holy Gaspel, before the undersigned Commissaire of the Superiour Court, declared and say:

    - That I am a Canadian Citizen .

That Mr. Bury Maurice who was born in Canada, and who is at Present in Austria directed by the address U.N.R.R.A. D.P.C. 148, Camp Landeck, Turol Austria-is my cousin.

    That his sincere wish to leave Europe and establish himself in Montreal Canada as soon as possible.

    That to give security to the Government of the Country where he has chosen to live, to the effect that he will have sufficient money to live independently, without being at the charge of the Government, I, the undersigned, bind and oblige myself to take care of my said cousin, to pay all the transportation fees, and to provide him with - sufficient money, for any other living expenses.

---   That my present wealth is approximatevily of $15.000.

    And I have signed at Montreal, Canada, this 25th day of April, 1946.

Ewdokia

Mrs Dora Babiak

Sworn to before me , at the City of Montreal, Canada, on this 25th,day of April, 1946.

R. R. Rhodes ?
....
Commissaire of the Superiour Court.

150

"What are you smiling about, Morrie?" Knight asked.

Maurice showed him the letter. "I am one step closer to home now."

"Huh. So you really are Canadian."

"Of course I am. I told you. I showed you my birth certificate."

Knight shrugged. "Those things can be forged. But mostly, it's your accent. You don't sound like a Canadian to me. You sound like a Russian. And you don't speak French."

"A lot of people from Canada don't speak French."

Corporal Knight responded with a half-smile and a wink.

There was another piece of paper in the envelope: a hand-written note from his Aunt Evdokia. It explained that she had sent a copy of the affidavit to the office of the Secretary of State in Ottawa, who when they approved Maurice's return to Canada, would send a telegram to the NRRA directorate in Austria. Maurice would then have to get permission and a ticket to travel to Vienna, where he could obtain security clearance from the Allied command.

He was one step closer. But there were still five to go.

Those steps took the second half of 1946. Governments never move quickly, and there were millions of D.P.s clamouring for emigration from Europe, especially from the USSR.

It was December 30, 1946, before a telegram arrived from the UNRRA office in Vienna.

rcd 30th December, 1946
Mr.Whitney-Coates
Mr.Knight
Camp Landeck

iamb v amu vienna nr.420

from   UNRRA Vienna 301620
to   UNRRA Innsbruck

bt

To Director French Zone Headquarters Innsbruck 599,
from Repatriation Officer Vienna.

Please arrange for Mr.Maurice BURY, Landeck
Camp, to come to Vienna soonest in order that security in
order that security clearance may be obtained here for his
journey to Canada.

(signed) C.S.MILLER

sent 301623 KWK
        ar
rcd 301630
IH   ar.

Then things sped up for Maurice. Corporal Knight helped him make applications, and pressured the commandant to sign papers.

Maurice celebrated New Year's Day 1947 with the GIs. He drank, he sang, and he danced with German, Czech and Polish girls at a party held in one of the barracks.

Two weeks later, Corporal Knight gave him a red bi-folded card, with a four-language title. It was an Allied Travel Permit that allowed him to go to Vienna. Ironically, the front was signed by the same French officer who had tried to send all the Ukrainians back to the U.S.S.R. in the fall—Charles Meistersheim.

Maurice paid for his train ticket out of the money he had saved from his meagre salary as a translator for the U.S. Army. Corporal Knight accompanied him to the train platform.

"So long, Morrie," he said, shaking Maurice's hand. "I'm glad you're going home. I hear we're going back stateside soon, too."

"Good. Thanks for all your help."

Knight waved his hand. "It was nothin'. But Morrie," he leaned closer, "if you want to convince people you're really from Canada, you better learn better English."

Vienna

February 1947

Maurice tucked the newspapers higher under his arm to draw his handkerchief from his pocket, and blew his nose for the thousandth time that day. *Five years of war, marching across whole countries, five years of sitting on cold and wet ground, of fighting and sheltering from bombs and bullets, of sneaking through the dark, and this is the worst I've ever felt.*

Except when the Germans were starving me in the prison camp.

Or when the Reds killed Kateryna.

He tucked away the handkerchief and turned up the collar on his coat, now badly worn and threadbare. Gusts came chilly and hard between the blasted buildings. Snow drifted against walls and slush clogged the streets. Postwar Vienna had more pressing concerns than snow clearing.

He turned a corner, and saw the three-man NKVD team in front of a bomb-damaged storefront. There was no mistaking the Soviet army's intelligence soldiers, with the red collars on the baby-shit brown coats, nor the lieutenant's blue peaked cap with the red band. The officer was arguing in broken German with a man in a torn coat, who held a hammer in one hand and a broken board in the other.

"There is no one like that here," the shopkeeper insisted. Like most Viennese in 1946, he was very thin. Maurice judged him to be about sixty years old. He had a grey fringe of hair around the back of his head, and despite the chilly air, no hat on his bald head. "No Russians, no Ukrainians."

Maurice kept walking at the same pace, hoping that the soldiers would not notice him. The three Ukrainian-language newspapers seemed to burn under his arm, even through the heavy winter coat he had taken from the German supply train all those months ago.

"Is very serious to hide Soviet deserter," he heard the lieutenant say behind him as he crossed the street.

The shopkeeper turned away and nailed the board up over the hole.

"We look inside," said the lieutenant, and stepped toward the door.

The shopkeeper jumped to block him. "No. You have no right to enter my shop," he said.

The NKVD soldiers lifted their rifles. "You think soldiers scare me now?" the shopkeeper said. "I've seen nothing but soldiers for the past ten years. Go away, Russian." He spat into the gutter.

Maurice pretended not to watch as he continued along the other side of the street. One of the soldiers pressed the barrel of his rifle into the shopkeeper's chest. "Go ahead, you son of a bitch," the shopkeeper growled. "You've already killed my son in Poland. You've destroyed my business. You may as well spill my blood, too. Pull the trigger, you Russian bastard."

A whistle echoed down the street, and against his will, Maurice turned. Two Vienna policemen ran toward the little tableau in front of the shop. The Soviet lieutenant looked disappointed. The soldiers drew their rifles across their chests and scowled as two young men in Vienna police uniforms approached.

Maurice turned away and walked as quickly as he thought he could without drawing attention to himself. He stepped into an alley and shoved the Ukrainian publications under a fallen chunk of masonry. He could easily replace them at the meeting he was heading to. He knew of close to forty Ukrainian-language publications produced in Vienna for the thousands of Ukrainians living in the city in 1946. They were refugees and emigrants, some living in U.N. displaced persons camps near the city. But there were also thousands who had emigrated before the war, and thousands more who had been born in Austria to immigrant parents.

And now, the NKVD were rounding up as many as they could to take back to the Ukrainian Soviet Socialist Republic. They didn't care whether they took deserters, people who took the opportunity to flee communism when they could, people who ran from the destruction of war, or Austrian citizens.

Or Canadian-born ethnic Ukrainians who had moved to Poland before Hitler and Stalin had divided the country between them.

As he stepped over a snow bank, he looked back at the shop. The shopkeeper stood, hammer in hand, watching the Vienna cops encouraging the NKVD men to move on.

A truck from the British army rumbled past the storefront where the defiant owner was still hammering. The NKVD and the Vienna police were gone.

Maurice blew his nose into a tattered handkerchief and walked faster to the meeting of the Ukrainian Central Relief Bureau, which he had read about in one Ukrainian-language weekly the day before. Set up by occupying Canadian and American soldiers of Ukrainian descent, the Bureau used its military access to almost anything they wanted, including D.P. camps, to provide food, clothing and counselling to Ukrainians. It operated at the edges of the laws and regulations of the U.N., which still did not recognize Ukraine as a distinct country—even though Stalin had demanded, and got, separate seats in the U.N. General Assembly for Ukraine and Belorussia.

Maurice arrived at the bomb-damaged church where the Central Ukrainian Relief Bureau, based in Innsbruck, had organized a meeting for Ukrainians living in Vienna who wanted to emigrate to western countries. Wiping his nose one more time, he pushed open the cracked, heavy door and stepped inside, realizing it was the first time he had been inside a church in over a year.

There must have been a hundred people sitting in the pews, while in front of the sacristy across the front of the church, a man in a Canadian Army uniform, another in a U.S. Army Air Force officer's uniform and a man in an Austrian tailored suit sat in wooden chairs.

"The USSR has set up the Soviet Administration of the Plenipotentiary for Repatriation Affairs in cities all across their zones of control in Germany and Austria," the American was saying in accented Ukrainian. "They are sending back to the USSR anyone they decide is Russian, Ukrainian or White Russian. Whether they want to go 'home' or not."

"They are also taking Latvian, Estonians and Lithuanians," said the Canadian, in better Ukrainian. "I doubt that Stalin is going to give up the Baltics or any other territory the Soviets conquered."

"They're also taking Ukrainian and Russian people who lived in Vienna before the war," said a middle-aged woman in the second pew. "There was a family next door to me. Their house was destroyed by the shelling. They were staying in a United Nations shelter, and the Red Army took them with refugees back to Ukraine. The soldiers didn't listen when they explained that they had lived in Vienna for years, that they were citizens of Austria even before the annexation. They didn't even care that the children were born in Austria."

"I saw them take a big group from a camp," said a short young man in the pews. "And the British soldiers were helping them, too."

"The Allies have agreed that all displaced persons should be repatriated," said the man in the suit, in clear, elegant Ukrainian. "However, the communists are the most intent about taking 'their' people back, and they're also more willing to use the laws to define anyone they want as Soviet citizens."

"How—" someone began, interrupted by a huge sneeze that echoed off the pews and the church's stone walls. Maurice felt his cheeks tingle as he wiped his face and hand with his handkerchief. "Pardon me," he said.

"God bless you," said a tiny, dark-haired woman sitting in the front pew.

The rest of the gathering looked at him for a moment, then apparently decided he was, in his nondescript coat and battered hat with the word "Canada" stitched to the front, not that interesting.

A young man in the congregation reported how Soviet Army soldiers carrying rifles came into a D.P. camp and ordered Ukrainian women and children onto trucks. "They were all crying," he said. He hung his head and Maurice could see a tear slip down his cheek. "I hid. I had to, or they would have taken me. I've been hiding ever since."

The two men in uniform at the front of the meeting described how the CURB was distributing food, clothing and other supplies, despite the official protests of the U.N. The small man in the dark suit described the vague efforts to intercede with official institutions to appeal for the rights of people who did not want to go back to the USSR, to stay in Austria and Germany, or emigrate to the United States or Canada.

As he said "America," the young man who had watched his friends taken away looked up, his eyes wide and shining. "How can I go to America?" he asked.

"Do you have any relatives there?" The American Air Force officer asked.

The young man shook his head, his lips quivering but hope still lurking in his eyes.

"Immigration is not easy," said the officer. "The U.S. is complying with the U.N. declaration, and the first priority is returning all displaced persons to their countries of origin." A groan rose from the congregation.

"That is not to say that it is impossible," said the man in the suit, holding his hands up. He stood. "There are steps and options for emigration in some circumstances," he said loudly, over the disappointed chatter of the crowd. "You can work with our officials and volunteers, but please remember, it can take time to get the authorization to travel out of Austria."

"And in the meanwhile, the communists take more of us back to Russia every day," said the young man who had spoken earlier. He rose to his feet and shouted: "What are you going to do about that? You soldiers, you Canadians and Americans, you're helping the Russians! What are you going to do?"

People near him hushed him, pulling on his sleeve to get him to sit down, but he shook his arm free. "You talk about administrative processes and circumstance, but our only circumstance is that we're freezing and starving until the communists find us and take us back to the Soviet Union." He pushed his way past the others on the pew beside him and strode out of the church. The closing door echoed.

The rest of the people gathered in the pews shook their heads and commented about the young man's hot temper. The three men at the front took command of the meeting again, trying to reassure the people that they were doing their best to look out for the Ukrainians in Vienna.

Maurice did not listen. He wiped his nose yet again, waiting for the meeting to conclude. When it finally did, he made his way to the front where the man in the suit was handing out leaflets to people as they left.

"You mentioned circumstances that could help with obtaining travel authorization to Canada," he said. "Would being a Canadian citizen be one of those circumstances?"

The man in the suit was very short and quite thin. He wore round, wire-rimmed glasses on a thin, pinched-looking nose, and his dark hair was carefully trimmed and combed and oiled. He looked up at Maurice, frowning. "How did you come to have Canadian citizenship?" he asked as he continued to pass out pamphlets.

"I was born in Canada."

"Then you should have no trouble. But how is it you are here in Vienna?"

Maurice could not just blurt out that he had come to Vienna from the USSR by way of Lithuania, Prussia and Berlin as a soldier in the Red Army. He had no way of knowing who might be a communist informer or spy in the church. Maybe even this dapper man made enough money as a paid informer for the Soviets that he could afford such an expensive, tailored suit in the midst of the postwar shortages. Maurice was about to begin the complex story he had devised, but as he opened his mouth, another sneeze caught him. This time, he managed to bring his handkerchief into place in time.

That was followed by a coughing fit. The small woman who had first blessed Maurice after his previous sneeze came up, concern on her face. She took Maurice by the elbow and led him to a pew at the side of the church. "Sit down. This is the warmest place in this church."

"Thank you," Maurice managed to croak between coughs.

The small woman put the back of her hand against Maurice's forehead, then his cheek. "At least you don't have a fever. Not yet, at any rate," she said. Maurice sneezed again and closed his eyes as the woman touched his face. It was the first tender touch he had felt in over a year.

Maurice sneezed again, but at least it was into his handkerchief this time. "That's it. You come home with us tonight."

"But I have a home," Maurice said.

"I have a cure for that cold. It works every time. Doesn't it, Andrei?" she said, turning to the man from the front of the room. He nodded.

"Andrei Hretsyk," he said, holding out his hand. "This is my wife, Yulia."

Maurice shook Hretsyk's hand and told them his name. He managed to hold in a sneeze.

"It seems you need more than one kind of help," Hretsyk said, laughing.

Outside the church, the streets were still almost as dark in the winter evening of 1947 as they had been during the blackouts. Few of Vienna's streetlights were working yet.

The Hretsyks led Maurice to the American zone, breezing past the American Army checkpoint with a smile and a wave at the GIs.

Maurice was almost shocked to see that their apartment building had suffered no visible damage. It felt like years since he had seen a building without scars of bombs or bullets.

The Hretsyks' apartment was larger than any he had seen in Poland or Ukraine. Late afternoon sunlight filtered through curtains over tall windows, bathing the dark wooden furniture in warm light.

Yulia Hretsyk led Maurice into a narrow kitchen, where the wooden cupboards had been painted bright white. She sat him in front of a similarly painted wooden table. As she waited for a kettle to boil on the gas stove, Andrei took a plain bottle from one of the cupboards and poured a shot of clear liquid into a small glass. Then he shook pepper into the glass and put it in front of Maurice. "Drink this."

Maurice's nose was so congested he could not detect an odour from the glass, not even of pepper. "What is it?" he asked.

"My own cure for the common cold." Andrei smiled, his eyes twinkling. "Gin and pepper."

Maurice picked up the glass, but hesitated before drinking. "Does it work?"

Andrei's smile got a little wider. "Who knows? But after a few treatments, you won't care." He laughed loudly, slapping his knee.

"Oh, Andrei," Yulia clucked as the kettle began to sing.

Maurice threw the concoction into his mouth and swallowed it fast. He could taste pepper and the perfume flavour of gin, but he barely registered the burning of the alcohol in his throat.

Andrei was about to pour another shot, but Yulia took the bottle from his hand. "That's enough for now. There is no reason to get a young man drunk quickly." She put a large bowl of steaming water on the table in front of Maurice. "Lean over and breathe in the steam," she ordered. As Maurice complied, she covered his head and the bowl with a towel. "Stay under there and just breathe until the water stops steaming."

Maurice closed his eyes. The steam around his face soothed him. Gradually, he could feel air penetrate though his nose again. He realized his head had been hurting for hours as the pain lessened. The alcohol had loosened the phlegm in his throat, too. Even his chest felt better, more relaxed, and the muscles in his neck and shoulders relaxed.

Then, disaster. A sneeze erupted out of his nose and mouth, splashing into the bowl in front of him. Mortified and disgusted, Maurice wiped his face with the towel before he pulled it off his head. His face was a dark red, as much from embarrassment as the steam.

Yulia smiled as she gingerly picked up the bowl, dumped the contents into the sink without looking at it, and proceeded to wash it. She then took the towel, careful not to touch any part where Maurice had wiped his face on it, and took it to a laundry hamper.

Andrei poured another gin and pepper for Maurice while his wife was out of the kitchen, and quickly another shot of gin without pepper for himself. "Now tell me your story," he said. "I cannot help you get to Canada if you don't."

All the hesitation and fear Maurice had felt evaporated like the steam in Yulia's bowl. For some reason, Maurice knew he could trust this couple. He began his story at the beginning.

Maurice told them how his ethnically Ukrainian parents had immigrated to Canada from Ternopyl even before the First Great War, and how he had been born in Montreal in 1919. How the family's once-thriving business had begun to flounder during the Depression, and how they had decided that his mother, Tekla, would return to the farm they still owned in Poland, where at least they had food to eat, while Michael remained in Canada to try to rebuild the business.

How in 1939, Nazi Germany and the communist USSR had divided Poland between them, with the Soviets taking over the eastern portion, including Lwow and Tarnopil, expelling the Poles and renaming the cities L'viv and Ternopyl, respectively.

As he spoke, Yulia began preparing a meal, with Andrei helping occasionally. "You'll eat with us, and stay the night, too," Yulia said.

"But I've already eaten," Maurice protested, thinking of the two slices of plain bread and slice of ham fat he had eaten before the meeting. Meagre, but not much else was available in Vienna in 1947 to a man unattached to any army.

Yulia ignored Maurice and with her husband's occasional help, bustled in the kitchen, silencing Maurice's protests with a wave of her hand.

He did not tell his new benefactors about being drafted in 1941, made an officer and thrown against Operation Barbarossa. He didn't tell them about the horrifying losses of the Red Army as it retreated across Ukraine and Russia before the German juggernaut, nor about being captured and starved in a German POW camp. He didn't tell Andrei and Yulia about escaping, with the 12 men under his command, and making his way home in German-occupied Ukraine, nor about joining the underground resistance movement of the Ukrainian Insurgent Army under Taras

Bulba-Borovets. The fewer people who knew about that, the safer he would be.

But he told them how, when the Soviets destroyed the stubborn German defence of Ternopyl—along with the whole city itself in 1944, they then drafted him into the Red Army. He told Andrei and Yulia how he had walked across the Baltic States and Poland to Germany, driving the shattered Wehrmacht out of the territory they had conquered. He told them a little about the grinding final battle to take Berlin. And he told them how he had gone to the British, who were still administering Canadian foreign affairs in Europe, asking for help to return home. "And the stupid officer told me to ask the Russians. He said he was certain they would give me the authorization to leave the army and go to Canada. The idiot."

"So you left the army?" Andrei asked. "Technically, that's desertion."

"I know. That's why I try to stay away from the Russians as much as I can. It's also why I put the 'Canada' tag on my hat."

"Yes. If the Soviets took you, they'd shoot you," said Andrei.

"Why did you come to Vienna?" Yulia asked as Andrei set the table. "Why not go west, where the British and Americans are in charge, instead of Vienna, which is divided among the four powers like Berlin?"

"When I left Berlin, I headed south toward the Americans. In Munich, I found a D.P. camp, but because I told them I'm Canadian, they said I was not eligible for help. But then I found work in an American kitchen. Later, I worked for them as a translator. From there, I got in touch with my family in Montreal. Finally, I got permission to come to Vienna. I hoped I might be able to find some organization or government agency that could help me get back home. To Canada, I mean. Montreal."

Yulia set out a simple Ukrainian meal: *perohe*, dumplings stuffed with potatoes, other with shredded cabbage. "It's still almost impossible to find meat and many other foods in Vienna," Andrei said. "But I hear that some parts in Germany are actually starving."

After dinner, Andrei poured each of them a small glass of apricot schnapps and they sat in the living room. He opened one of the tall windows to let in some of the cool night breeze, but closed it soon after when Yulia began to shiver. "You were right to come to Vienna," Andrei said, sipping the drink. "The victorious powers have separated Austria and Germany. They are determined never to let the two countries join again. Which means there will soon be formal embassies and government-to-government representation here. And that means you will have someone to ask for a travel permit."

The Hretsyks made up a bed on their living room sofa for Maurice, and after a final shot of gin and pepper, Maurice fell asleep, waking only when Andrei shook his shoulder. He had pulled back the curtains, and the weak autumn daylight showed him wearing another pressed, if slightly out of date suit, crisp white shirt and elegant tie.

"What time is it?" Maurice asked.

"Seven a.m. I'm going to work now. I'll walk with you to your hotel."

They breakfasted on Viennese bread and Moka, Viennese coffee. Mrs. Hretsyk kissed her husband goodbye at the apartment building door on the street, and Maurice and Andrei strolled through the cold February streets.

The Hretsyks' neighbourhood was surprisingly undamaged, but after only a few blocks, they came to an area that had been almost completely destroyed. Maurice looked at skeletons of apartments, buildings reduced to piles of bricks, walls that rose with blank spots where windows used to be and ended in uneven tops, open to the dull grey sky.

Andrei walked with Maurice to the door of the Hotel Schweizerhof, in the centre of Vienna, the sector occupied jointly by all four powers—the U.S., USSR, Britain and

France. Built at the turn of the century, its exterior walls had once been white, but now were smudged and grey with the detritus of battle. Still, it had suffered relatively little damage, and the staff kept the sidewalk in front of the door clear of snow. The United Nations Relief and Rehabilitation Administration, UNRRA, had taken it over for temporary housing for its people—and in Maurice's case, for refugees awaiting transfer.

Maurice said goodbye to Andrei Hretsyk at the door. He asked the desk clerk, who looked far too weary for his twenty years, whether there were any messages for him. The clerk barely glanced at the cubby hole before shaking his head no and tossed the room key onto the counter.

His two roommates were nearly ready to go out for their day of hounding various officials for travel authorization. Wojtek was shaving when Maurice walked in, while Zoltan, from Hungary, was sitting on the end of his bed, tying his shoes.

"Where did you go last night? Anyone I know?" said Wojtek. He was from western Poland, hoping to emigrate to the U.S.

Maurice sneezed again, wishing for more gin and pepper. "I stayed with some Ukrainian people who have lived in Vienna for twenty years," he said.

"Did you learn anything useful?" Zoltan asked. He didn't care where he could travel to, as long as it was out of the reach of the NKVD.

"The people I stayed with may be able to help me get travel authorization. It's the last thing I need." He sat down on the end of his own bed.

The room had been designed and constructed as a single room, but the UNRRA had applied some arcane formula and determined that three men could stay in it. Three cots pressed against each other and the walls. They had to lean Maurice's cot against the wall to open the wardrobe, and slide sideways to get around the other cots.

Maurice sneezed again, barely getting his handkerchief out in time. His roommates shook their heads and squeezed past him, out to try to find work, money, food and some way to get out of Europe.

When the door closed, Maurice flopped back onto the cot. He was still tired, his head still hurt and he was still wracked with sneezing. He wished for some more gin and pepper. He could not tell whether it had helped the night before, but as Andrei Hretsyk had said, after a couple of treatments, he didn't care.

He turned up the dial on the steam radiator under the window, careful that the sheet on Zoltan's cot wasn't touching it. He looked at the grey slush on the sill outside the window and shivered. He decided to try Yulia's treatment. He pushed his cot up against the wall and took the tiny electric hotplate from the wardrobe. The electricity in Vienna had been fairly consistent since he had arrived, which was a huge improvement over the coil-stove heated barracks in Camp Kufstein.

After a few minutes, he had a kettle boiling. He covered his head with his second shirt to try to capture the steam and breathed slowly. After a while, he started to feel his sinuses opening up. The pain in his forehead diminished.

There was a knock at the door, and Maurice realized he had fallen asleep on the cot. "Why do you have a shirt over your head?" asked Andrei Hretsyk when Maurice opened the door.

"Oh—I was using your wife's treatment again," Maurice said, confused and embarrassed. He threw the shirt onto his bed. "What are you doing here?"

Hretsyk still looked elegant, with his suit and shirt immaculate. He held his dark grey fedora in one hand and his thin leather briefcase in the other. "I have good news for you. I have found a British officer who can sign your travel permit."

"Travel to where?"

"Canada."

Maurice's heart pounded. He stood still, mouth slightly open, eyes wide. He could not breathe for several seconds, and it wasn't because of his cold.

"Well? Come on. He's in the British sector, at their headquarters. "

Maurice grabbed his coat and battered hat with the "Canada" tag still clinging to it and followed Andrei out of the hotel. "What time is it?"

"It's after two."

I slept over four hours. Maurice also realized he was hungry, and his throat was dry as well as sore. He managed to persuade Andrei to stop at a little shop for a cup of tea, and drank it so fast it only made his throat even more painful.

They went south, out of the central part of the city which was under the rotating administration of the four occupying powers, toward the British-controlled Landstrasse district. Tiny snowflakes began to fall, swirling in the gusts between the shattered buildings of Vienna.

But before they could get to the Ringstrasse, the boundary of the central district, a battered, dirty Studebaker truck groaned up the street and slid to a messy stop in the snow beside Andrei and Maurice. A man jumped out of the passenger seat, and Maurice recognized the brown coats and red flashes of the NKVD.

He also recognized the NKVD officer from the storefront the day before.

"Halt!" the officer demanded. Behind him, three NKVD soldiers jumped out of the back of the truck. "Good afternoon, Mr. Hretsyk," he said in Russian.

"Good afternoon, officer. Please stand aside. I am in a hurry," Andrei said, but the Russian officer stopped him with a hand on his shoulder.

"We have been watching you, Mr. Hretsyk. We know you are helping Ukrainian refugees avoid repatriation."

Andrei stood up as tall as he could and looked the NKVD officer in the eye. "You don't know what you're talking about. Now get out of my way."

"This man is a deserter," said the officer. Maurice felt cold that had nothing to do with the falling snow. He felt like his body was hollow, empty inside, and he heard a rushing sound in his ears. "He is coming with us back to the Soviet Union."

Maurice blinked. The city of Vienna whirled in front of his eyes. *Not now. Not when I'm so close.*

"Don't be ridiculous," Andrei said. "This man is a Canadian citizen." He turned to Maurice and switched to English. "Show him your birth certificate, Maurice."

Maurice could not keep his hands from shaking as he reached inside his coat and drew out his tattered Dominion of Canada birth certificate. He unfolded it carefully, trying not to stress the creases any more. *What if this Russian takes it away from me?* he wondered.

The Russian officer took the worn paper carefully, frowning. "I cannot read Roman script."

"Then you will have to take my word for it," said Andrei. He took the birth certificate out of the Russian's hands and carefully gave it back to Maurice. Maurice's hands shook so much, he had trouble refolding it, and did not even try to put it away in his inner coat pocket.

"I don't have to take your word for anything," said the officer.

"Listen here," Andrei said, stepping between Maurice and the Russian. "You're still in the four-power zone, and now is not the USSR's turn to administer it. You have no right to arrest or deport anyone, let alone a citizen of an Allied country."

The Russian's hand went to his sidearm. "Who will stop me?"

Maurice's heart pounded so loudly in his ears, he could barely hear the argument. He knew the time had come for him to say something, so he stepped beside Andrei Hretsyk and spoke in the best English he could manage. "Is there something I can help you with? Are you looking for some information about Canada?"

The NKVD officer glared at him. "Yes. Tell me who's president of Canada," he said in heavily accented, but nearly fluent English.

Hopefully, he won't detect my accent. "There is no president of Canada. The Prime Minister is William Lyon Mackenzie King."

He took a deep breath. Speaking had calmed him, the roaring in his ears had stopped and he could think clearly. "Mr. Hretsyk and I are on our way to a meeting with the British Administration Command —" Does that sound plausible?—"and the UNRRA. We really do not have time to delay. If we do not get there on time, there will be official enquiries."

It was a fabrication, but it sounded officious enough that the NKVD officer's hand left his sidearm holster.

"Come, Herr Hretsyk." Maurice took Andrei's elbow and led him around the NKVD officer. "We must hurry," he continued in English. "You know how the colonel feels about ...tawdriness."

"That's 'tardiness,'" Andrei said under his breath as they put distance between themselves and the Russian—quickly, but not too quickly.

It took more than a half hour to reach the British headquarters in a sprawling, elegant 18th century mansion made of plaster-covered stones painted light green.

Andrei knew these men, too, and breezed past the guards and clerks until he stood in the office of Captain Philip C.L. Hildash, as indicated by an elegantly engraved sign on his ornate desk, made of cherry wood inlaid with other woods and carved in the eighteenth-century style. "I'm acting in a colonel's capacity," he said by way of explaining a question no one had asked. "I understand you come highly recommended, Mr. Retsick."

"It's Hretsyk," Andrei said, in English. "And you, I understand can authorize international travel."

"Indeed I can." He stood. Captain, Acting Colonel, Hildash was a tall, thin and very young officer with straw-coloured hair and large teeth. His bright blue eyes protruded slightly. "Where do you want to go, Mr. Restock?" He sat on the edge of his inlaid desk, one foot swinging.

"*Hretsyk*. And it's not I who needs to go to Canada. It's my good friend here, Maurice Bury."

Captain Hildash's eyebrows rose. "Canada? That's very far. Why should this man go to Canada?"

"Because he is a Canadian. Born in Canada. Repatriating him means returning him to Montreal."

Captain Hildash turned to Maurice. "I assume you can provide some kind of evidence to support this?"

Maurice pulled out his birth certificate for the second time that day, along with his red travel authorization signed by the commandant of Camp Landeck. Last, he took out the affidavit signed by his Aunt Evdokia in Montreal, where she promised to sponsor him and provide him with work, and the accompanying authorization from the Canadian Secretary of State, Louis St-Laurent.

Captain Hildash took the forms, spread them out on his desk and sat behind it. He stared hard at them and thought. He looked up at Maurice, then at Andrei and back at Maurice again, his bright blue eyes shining. He looked at the forms again and nodded. "Very well. You have clearance to travel within Austria. I can authorize you to exit the country, to travel all the way to Canada. But you will have to pay for your transit yourself."

"That is not a problem," Maurice said.

And a few minutes later, Maurice walked out of the British Occupational Headquarters in Vienna with two new documents: a red card, similar to the travel permit he got in Landek, that described him as an "interpreter student" born in Canada, filled out in Captain Hildash's peculiar square handwriting. For some reason that Maurice would never understand, Captain Hildash wrote down his birthdate incorrectly by one month, as "4 March 1919."

But most important, it authorized him to travel from Austria to Canada, any time between 7 February and 7 May,

1947. The clerk with corporal's stripes stamped "Allied Military Control, Vienna."

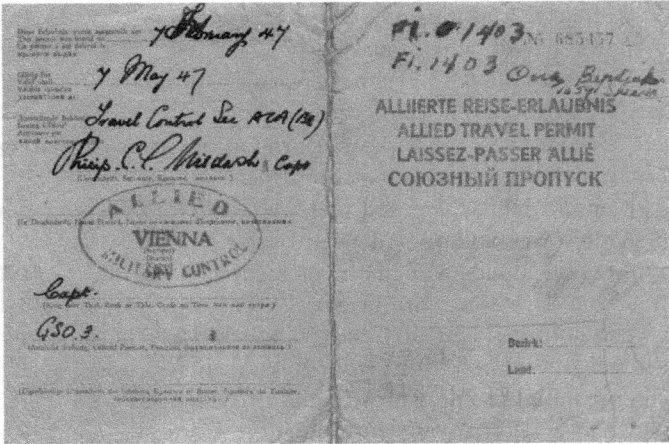

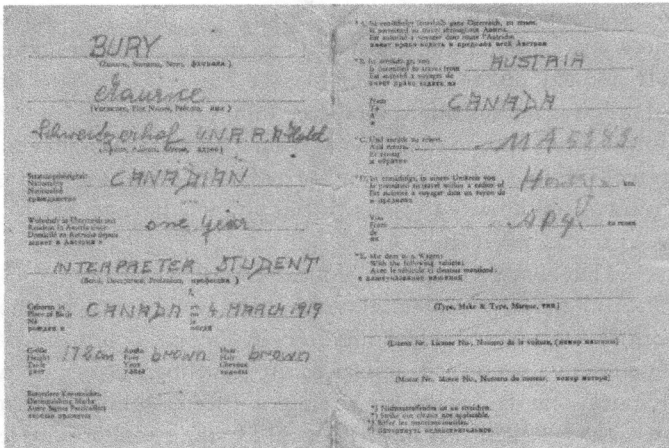

He also got a smaller green card, a Military Exit Permit that not only allowed him to leave Austria, but required him to cross the frontier 7 May, 1947.

MILITÄRISCHE AUSREISE-ERLAUBNIS Nr. 482

Military   Exit   Permit No.

Gilt nur in Verbindung mit dem gültigen Reisepass des Inhabers.
Only valid in conjunction with the bearer's valid passport.
Die Alliierten Militärbehörden ermächtigen die unten genannte Person die angegebene Reise zu unternehmen.
The Allied Military Authorities authorize the person named below to travel as stated.

1. Zuname .... BURY
   Surname
2. Vornamen .... Maurice
   Christian Names
3. Frühere Zunamen ....
   Other Surnames
4. Geburtsort und-Datum MONTREAL CANADA 7.3.19.
   Date and Place of Birth
5. Geschlecht .... MALE
   Sex
6. Gegenwärtige Staatsangehörigkeit ... CANADIAN
   Present Nationality
7. Personalausweis Bezw. Reisepass 290/47
   Identity Document or Passport
   (a) Nr. Ausstellungsort und-Datum LANDECK 9 I 47
       No. Date and Place of Issue
   (b) Ausstellungsbehörde ....
       Issuing Authority
   (c) Ablaufsdatum ....
       Date of Expiry
8. Begleitet von ....
   Accompanied by

9. Unterschrift des Inhabers ....
   Signature of Holder
10. Von den Alliierten Grenzebebörden auszufüllen
    To be filled in by the Allied Frontier Authorities

Date Left......... Date Returned.........

MILITÄRISCHE AUSREISE-ERLAUBNIS Nr. 482
Military Exit Permit No.

11. Von AUSTRIA Nach CANADA
From To

12. Reise: Einfach Rückfahrt Durchreise
Journey: Single Return Transit

13. Grenze muss überschritten werden vor 7 May 47
Frontier must be crossed before

14. Gültigkeitsdauer (Bei der Rückfahrt)
If return, period of validity

15. Grenzübergangsstelle (Anmeldungspflicht!)
Bezw. Lufthafen.
Compulsory frontier post or airport

Im namen der Alliierten Militärbehörden
For the Allied Military Authorities

Colonel
American General Staff

Colonel
British General Staff

Date

Date 7 Feb 47

Russian General Staff

Date

ALLIED MILITARY CONTROL
DATE ARR.
DATE DEP. 25 FEB 1947
VIENNA
SCHWECHAT

PSS A 4002 40M 2-45.

Two and a half weeks later, the green Exit permit received another stamp, at the Vienna Schwechat airport: Allied Military Control, Date Dep.: 25 Feb 1947.

Maurice had succeeded in walking out of war.

Epilogue

Maurice settled in Montreal with his father, Michael, but was unable to bring his mother and sister out of the USSR until 1970.

In Montreal, Maurice met a Ukrainian immigrant, the young Sophia Niunka from L'viv. They married in May, 1949. They bought a house in Verdun, a suburb of Montreal, as well as investment properties they rented out across the city.

Maurice soon found work as an electrical technician for Northern Electric, the company that eventually became Nortel. Fortunately, he retired long before the company's management drove it into financial excesses that led to its bankruptcy in the 21st century.

Maurice and Sophia had one child, a lovely daughter they named Roxanne. Smart *and* beautiful, after she graduated with her Honours Bachelor of Arts degree from Carleton University, she had the poor judgment to marry a hopeful writer from Thunder Bay.

Author's note

I feel very fortunate to have met and known Maurice Bury.

Walking Out of War is the third and concluding volume in the story of Maurice Bury's wartime experiences—but not of his life.

As mentioned in the last chapter, after the war, Maurice returned to his birthplace, Montreal. There he reunited with his father, Michael. And he went on to lead an extraordinary life in that extraordinary city. He built a career as an electrical technician, and married a Ukrainian immigrant, Sophia Niunka. They had a daughter, Roxanne, and built up some impressive real estate holdings.

Maurice also became a leader in the Ukrainian community in Montreal, holding the position of President of the Prosvita, the Taras Shevchenko Ukrainian Canadian Reading Society in Montreal, for over thirty years.

During his lifetime, Maurice was able to bring his mother out of the U.S.S.R. to live with him for a few years. Tekla Kuritsa returned to Ukraine, however, before the end of the 1970s and passed away in 1985.

In his life, Maurice was never one to bend your ears with stories about his experience in the war. But he would share some of them, if asked. As a father, he responded to complaints about school cafeteria food with tales about the truly horrible food he had to endure as a soldier and especially as a prisoner of war.

What Maurice did was to inspire those around him. He sparked value for education, interest in history and dedication to community—as well as a healthy dose of skepticism for politicians and anyone who would have us believe they have all the answers.

Maurice passed away at the end of 2004, at the age of 85. He is survived by his wife, Sophia, daughter Roxanne, and grandsons Evan and Nicolas. And his great-grandson is also his namesake: Maurice Lopez Bury was born in 2012.

Acknowledgements

Walking Out of War, like the previous volumes *Army of Worn Soles* and *Under the Nazi Heel*, would not have been possible without the help and support of a large number of people.

First, I have to thank Maurice, himself, for being an inspiration and for sharing his memories and knowledge.

Thanks to his daughter, my wife, Roxanne, for her memories of her father and for the love and support over these many years.

Thanks to Gary Henry for being such a professional, eagle-eyed and supportive editor—not just for finding problems, but for pointing to the best solution every time.

Thanks to beta readers Samreen Ahsan, Elise Stokes and Frederick Lee Brooke for making excellent suggestions and for pointing out errors and problems that I missed, even after going through the manuscript I can't tell you how many times.

Thanks to David C. Cassidy for another outstanding cover that captures the essence of the story perfectly. Again.

And thanks to Joy Lorton, the Typo-Detective, for proofreading so assiduously, professionally and efficiently.

This book just would not be as good as it is without all their help.

About the author

I am a journalist, editor and novelist based in Ottawa, Canada. After more than 20 years of writing for magazines and newspapers like *Macworld*, the *Financial Post, Applied Arts*, the Ottawa *Citizen* and *Graphic Arts Monthly*, I decided to publish my first writing love, fiction. I published a children's story, Sam, the Strawb Part in 2011. Later, I published an occult/paranormal short story for grown ups, Dark Clouds.

The Bones of the Earth came out in 2012. You might call it an epic fantasy, but I prefer the term that I made up, historical magic realism.

I followed that in 2013 with *One Shade of Red*, an erotic romantic spoof. In 2015, I entered the Kindle World of fan fiction, after being invited to write for Toby Neal's Lei Crime Kindle World and Russell Blake's JET Kindle World. I responded with *Torn Roots* and *Jet: Stealth*, respectively. Since then, I have published two more Lei Crime Kindle World books and a Sydney Rye Kindle World novella, *The Wife Line*. A fourth Lei Crime Kindle World novella, *Echoes*, will be released in May 2017.

The first volume in the true story of Maurice Bury, my father-in-law, *Army of Worn Soles*, hit the shelves in 2014. For a short time, it was #3 in the Military Memoirs in Canada category, behind Canadian supersoldier Cody Mitic's *Unflinching: The Making of a Canadian Sniper.*

Under the Nazi Heel is the second book in the series. It was published in February 2016.

In between writing books and blog posts, I've also helped found an author's cooperative publishing venture, Independent Authors International, and I am active in the author's professional association BestSelling Reads.

Let me know what you think, or if you have any questions, about any of my books. Contact me through my website, The Written Word (writtenword.ca), my blog, Written Words, and on Twitter @ScottTheWriter.

Books by Scott Bury

Army of Worn Soles (Maurice Bury volume 1)
Amazon ASIN B00L3CNE0M
ISBN 978-0-9879141-9-4
A Canadian is drafted into the Soviet Red Army during World War 2, just in time to be thrown against Nazi Germany's invasion in Operation Barbarossa.

Under the Nazi Heel (Maurice Bury volume 2)
Amazon ASIN B01C4PZW2O
ISBN 978-1-987846-01-0

To protect his family, Maurice Bury joins the secret resistance against the brutal German occupation of Ukraine. He soon finds himself facing more than the Germans: Soviet spies, the Polish Home Army and enemies even closer to home.

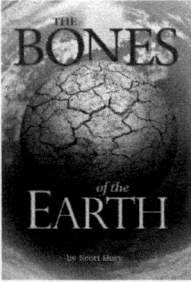

The Bones of the Earth (The Dark Age, Book 1)
Amazon ASIN B006PI0NRG
ISBN 978-0-9879141-1-8

Rejected by his own people, pursued by a dragon, young Javor heads for Constantinople, the centre of civilization, during the darkest time of the Dark Age.

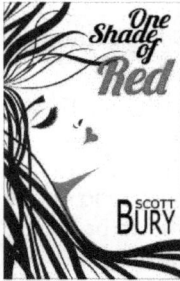

One Shade of Red
Amazon ASIN B00C28NLJA
ISBN

Women want the perfect man, so they can change him. But when university student Damian Serr discovers a rich, beautiful woman who's voracious about sex, he doesn't try to improve on perfection.

Sam, the Strawb Part
Amazon ASIN B005NFHASM
ISBN 978-0-9869529-2-0

What happens when a thin boy dresses as a pirate, attaches a jolly roger to his bicycle and starts to hijack strawberries?

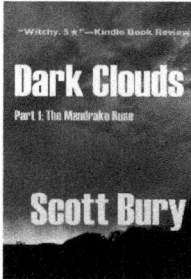

Dark Clouds: The Mandrake Ruse
Amazon ASIN B005X3A6YE
ISBN 978-0-9869529-3-7

As the Witch's Son, Matt and his pretty wife are drawn into a spider's web.

Lei Crime Kindle World titles

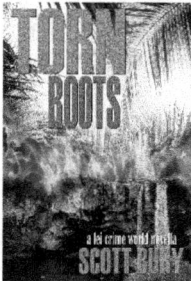

Torn Roots
Amazon ASIN B012PK5HJ6

As environmentalists, property developers, protesters, arsonists, kidnappers and a rogue Homeland Security agent converge on Hana, Maui, Detective Pono Kaihale and FBI Special Agent Vanessa Storm turn to a brilliant young geologist for answers.

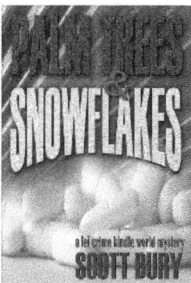

Palm Trees & Snowflakes
Amazon ASIN B019NR16H6

Snowflake has a whole new meaning in Hawaii. The new designer drug being trafficked through Oahu gives users the perfect high—and slowly kills them.

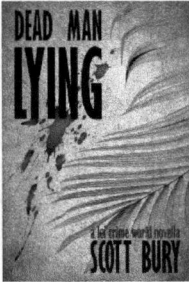

Dead Man Lying
Amazon ASIN: B01HBVUR8K

With lush rain forests, black sand beaches, and a laid-back lifestyle, Maui offers the perfect retirement location for once-famous country singer Steven Sangster … until he ends up dead.
Detective Lei Texeira and FBI Special Agent Vanessa Storm must untangle the lies before the music dies.

Echoes (coming May 2017)
A secret from Vanessa Storm's past sets off consequences that echo through the decades—with deadly consequences.

Jet Kindle World titles
Jet: Stealth
Amazon ASIN B012P698K4

Once Mossad's deadliest assassin, Jet is headed for a new, quiet life in a tropical paradise. When a mysterious, handsome agent with no tradecraft but with brilliant blue eyes asks for her help to secure a new stealth weapon, she finds she just can't say no.

Sydney Rye Kindle World titles

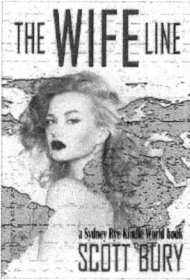

The Wife Line
Amazon ASIN B01D281RBC

Human traffickers are selling young women from eastern Europe as sex slaves and killing them when they become inconvenient. Sydney Rye's job is only to protect her client, until a mysterious, aggravating and irresistible young crusader pulls her and Blue on a far more dangerous path: taking down the whole slaving ring.

www.ingramcontent.com/pod-product-compliance
Lightning Source LLC
Chambersburg PA
CBHW072019060426
42446CB00044B/2803